The Director in the Theatre

By the same author

OLD VIC PREFACES

The Director in the Theatre

by

HUGH HUNT

Routledge and Kegan Paul

LONDON

First published 1954
by Routledge and Kegan Paul Ltd.
Broadway House, Carter Lane, E.C.4
Made and printed in Great Britain
by William Clowes and Sons, Limited
London and Beccles

Contents

120592

Foreword

IN a country which has the richest store of dramatic writing in the world, it is a sad reflexion on our public attitude to the arts that only one of our Universities should be prepared to make a serious study of the Art of the Theatre. Yet the fact that Bristol should be the first to house a Department of Drama is an indication of the interest in the theatre which is developing in the provinces.

A healthy theatrical tradition must have deeper roots than the West End theatre can provide if it is to grow and prosper. Perhaps one of the most encouraging things about our British theatre is the repertory movement which is growing up throughout the country. This, surely, is the proof that the theatre is laying foundations for its future. Those who have seen the work of the Department of Drama at Bristol will, I feel sure, join with me in the desire to see other Universities follow suit. For the surest guarantee of an intelligent and live theatre is the creation of an appreciative and critical audience. Moreover, the study of the theatre, which it is the privilege of this University to provide, is a valuable educational medium.

In a world which is becoming increasingly ruled by the machine; where science and economics are the dominant factors in the life of man; more than ever do we need the special properties of the arts to leaven our bread. In the study of the theatre the student will find more than an average share of the humanities represented. In it he will find the history of literature, the beauty of language, the mysteries of man's thought and beliefs and, above all, the study of man himself—his manners, his beliefs, his faults, his courage and his essential lovableness. These, I believe, are fit studies for the arts faculty of a University to foster.

Four of the lectures in this book are the result of the Rocke-feller Foundation Lectures which I was invited to deliver at Bristol University to the students of the Drama Department and to the students of the Bristol Old Vic School of Acting during the session of 1953–4. The chapter on contemporary Shakespeare Production was delivered as a Bergen Lecture at Yale University in May, 1954.

When I was invited to lecture on the work of the producer —or director as I have preferred to call him in this book—I was honoured and troubled. Honoured because the Depart-ment of Drama at Bristol University and the Bristol Old Vic School grew up side by side with the Bristol Old Vic Theatre, with the development of which I was somewhat connected; troubled because in trying to assemble my thoughts on play direction I realised, for the first time, the extent of the director's responsibilities to the theatre. I realised, moreover, that although much has been said about the technicalities of play direction, there is no informative handbook on how to visualise a play, nor on the precise limits of a director's influence on the script, the actors and the audience. The more I thought about these things, the more I realised that there can be no satisfactory explanation of the process of play interpretation, nor can we set a boundary to the director's influence. The degree of a director's work will vary from play to play and must ulti-mately depend on the personality of the director himself. In fact we can no more explain how a play should be directed than we can explain how to paint a picture of the Crucifixion. We can teach the student of painting how to mix his paints, how to set up his canvas, how to choose his light and what sort of brushes to use; but how to interpret his subject—

that is something which lies outside the province of the teacher.

The production of a play is an act of creative interpretation. Purists may object that interpretation should not be creative, and claim that the trouble with most play directors is that they cannot restrain their imagination. But, then, purists will never make satisfactory directors. Purism and play directing do not go hand in hand, and the best directors are those who most often break the rules.

In these chapters I have said little about the technicalities of production, which have been treated elsewhere. I have said little about the rules. Yet, there must be a thread of reason— something we can hold on to—in the creative interpretation of a play. It is this thread that I have tried to pursue in the following chapters. It may be no more than an attitude towards the theatre—a respect for its proprieties, a kindliness towards its participants, a love for its traditions and a burning desire for its welfare.

I am conscious of my inability to make my analysis of the director's craft and responsibilities as clear as it might be, but I am grateful to the Universities of Bristol and Yale for giving me the opportunity to try.

Brockenhurst, 1954.

The Director and the Art of the Theatre

IT was suggested that I choose as a title for these lectures the Art of the Director. I have declined to do so, not out of modesty in respect of my calling, but because I believe there should be no such thing. The art the director serves is the Art of the Theatre, and this is a composite art; the author, the actors, the director, the designer and the technicians are its practitioners. Yet acting and play-writing are independent arts, and are often to be seen in circumstances which could not by any stretch of the imagination be called theatrical art. The great classical and romantic actors of the 18th, 19th and early 20th centuries provided examples of virtuoso acting, which sometimes rose to the heights of art, though the composite performance of the plays in which they appeared was often deplorable. The art of play-writing is, of course, self-evident, and we can often appreciate the genius of Shakespeare better in the study than on the stage.

But the Art of the Theatre is a rarer experience than that of play-writing and play-acting. It is the perfect synthesis of all the ingredients that go to make up that illuminating experience we call the theatre. This experience is not necessarily dependent on superb performances by the actors, nor on the literary brilliance of the writing. The court masques of Ben Jonson and

Inigo Jones were neither great literature nor did they allow scope for great acting, yet in performance they were surely works of singular beauty. *The Miracle* staged by Reinhardt was a more important theatrical experience than *Hamlet* staged by the local 'rep.'

In effect, a performance of *Hamlet* can be either a work of theatrical art, or a dismal fiasco. The Art of the Theatre, then, rests not alone on literary, nor on histrionic art; though both these, I believe, must be amongst the ingredients. It rests upon the effectiveness of the total composition; and for this composition, the director is, or can be, the decisive factor.

But in maintaining there is no such thing as a separate art of direction, I do not suggest that the director should not consider himself an artist, I believe he is, or should be, an artist of the theatre. His task is to serve the composite, rather than seek to display an individual artistry. His duty is to create the conditions in which the Art of the Theatre can thrive.

We often seem to be dealing with intangibles when we talk of the Art of the Theatre. Each of us is reasonably sure what he means by it, but, like a performance of music, it is easier to feel than to analyse. What we must first bear in mind is that for theatrical art to exist, all its component parts must be of theatrical value. The script may be of literary value or it may not; what matters is that it should be of theatrical value. Tennyson's *Becket*, Byron's *Manfred*, Shelley's *Cenci*, Browning's *Strafford*, may be valuable works of literature, but having little or no theatrical value they are unlikely to be satisfactory components of theatrical art. The same principle holds good of the scenery and costumes, which must not only be artistically satisfying, but theatrically satisfying as well. This principle is no less true of the acting, for the greatest difficulty that confronts the actor is not merely how to find the truth of a character, but how to make that truth theatrical.

If we hold fast to this good word theatrical, not in its debased usage as meaning something false, but in its pure sense of belonging to the theatre, we stand on surer ground. But not altogether so; for in the Art of the Theatre—as in all arts—contradictions are also true, and a writer or an actor who aims only at theatrical values is unlikely to achieve theatrical art. Theatricalism must be married to truth—must, in fact, give birth to a child of its own, which we call theatrical truth, if it is to weave the spell that we may safely call the Art of the Theatre.

We must not, however, confuse this truth with realism any more than we should consider that theatrical art must necessarily be based on poetic writing or philosophic, social or moral content. Theatrical art may contain any of these things, but it is first and foremost an art form in its own right; and what distinguishes it from any other art is its own peculiar life force, which we may call theatrical truth. On the stage a spade is no longer of value as a spade, it is only valuable if it is a theatrical spade. A theatrical spade may only be made of wood, and the grave that we dig with it may only be a trap-door, but what matters is that the imagination with which we endow it is correctly conceived in terms of theatrical effect.

> 'What's Hecuba to him, or he to Hecuba,
> That he should weep for her?'

Hamlet asks after seeing an actor perform his part. The answer is, of course, that the actor has created a theatrical effect. He has invested Hecuba with theatrical truth, and it is because of this truth that we, and the actor, can weep. But we need more than a variety of components endowed with theatrical truth to create an art. We require a synthesis of all these things—and this synthesis must be endowed with a vision. To create the conditions in which the Art of the Theatre can thrive, the director must create this synthesis and conceive this vision.

I believe that in discussing this question we can keep our feet

3

on the ground. The theatre, like all the arts, is more easily analysed by practice than by theory, and what we see when we go to it, and what we do when we act in it, is of infinitely greater value than what we can say or write of it. Yet for all its mystique, its emotions, its ephemeral existence, the play on the stage is nine-tenths a matter of craftsmanship, planning and clear thinking. There remains the fraction—the one-tenth—which is the soul as opposed to the body of a production. The body is the exposition of the story of the play, the clarification and clash of the characters, the skilful use of costumes, scenery, lighting, music and movement; what remains to be found is the reason why all these things happen in the way they do, and this is the soul. Now this soul is the result of the vision of some person or persons, and this vision must be endowed with theatrical truth. More often than not the vision does not exist, or is not endowed with theatrical truth, or this truth is so weak that it fails to convince us. Perhaps the acting is good and the play good, but the total effect does not inspire us. Only when we leave the theatre inspired and elevated, not merely by the author and actor but by the existence of the theatre itself, can we say we have witnessed the Art of the Theatre.

It would be helpful if I could give concrete, contemporary examples of this art, but I am aware that the examples I can give are of doubtful effect. We have not all seen the same productions. Moreover, the experience of a work of art is an individual experience, depending on our mood when we see it. We are not all inspired when we first see the Mona Lisa of Da Vinci. We may have our minds on other things, or we may be so footsore from walking round the Louvre that our only reaction is to scowl at that serenely smiling lady. But at least with a picture or a statue or a piece of literature we can, if we wish, go back and revisit them when conditions are more favourable to our critical faculties. But the best theatre is short-lived, and we can rarely find time to revisit the same production of a play to confirm or modify our first impressions.

4

I can, then, only give examples of productions which, at the time that I saw them, convinced me that the theatre is, or can be, a complete and absolute art form. There was Bertolt Brecht's production of his own play *Mother Courage* in Berlin; Elia Kazan's production of *Tea and Sympathy* in New York; Peter Brook's production of *Dark of the Moon* at the Lyric, Hammersmith; Jean Vilar's production of *Le Cid* for the Théâtre National Populaire in Paris; Reinhardt's production of *Jederman* at Salzburg; a tradition production of *Juno and the Paycock* at the Abbey Theatre with F. J. McCormick, Barry Fitzgerald, Eileen Crowe and Maureen Delaney; Michel St. Denis's production of *The Three Sisters*. These, among others, are my masterpieces. My theatrical experience is, of course, limited, and I make no claim to a comprehensive survey of contemporary theatre. I merely quote examples of productions that have represented for me works of theatrical art. But whether we can all agree on any of the examples I have quoted or not, I hope we can at least agree on the fact that, despite much that is bad and even contemptible in theatrical presentation, there is such a thing as the Art of the Theatre, which exists not necessarily dependent on, but complementary to, the Art of the Actor and the Dramatist.

I said that this art demanded the synthesis of a number of component parts, each endowed with theatrical truth, and that this synthesis must be welded together by the vision brought to it by the director. But the director is a comparative new-comer to the theatre. Up to the end of the 19th century no such functionary appears on the playbills or is known for certain to have existed behind the scenes. Are we then to sup-pose that prior to his arrival there was no such thing as the Art of the Theatre?

The suggestion is, of course, absurd. The author is often the best judge of how his play is to be performed. The actor will often know best how to perform it. I have no doubt that authors like Shakespeare and Molière were able to create many examples of theatrical art; whilst among contemporary actors, Gielgud, Olivier, Barrault, Gründgens and Alfred Lunt have achieved composite productions which were more than mere exhibitions of their personal art of acting. But, although complementary, it does not follow that the arts of acting and playwriting are easily co-ordinated. It is this task of co-ordinating the various elements that primarily gave birth to the director in the theatre. At the lowest he is the referee who stops the fouls between the two principal parties; at the highest he is the man who welds together the theatrical verities of author, actor, designer and technician, and unifies all these by his vision.

In performing the task of welding the components, the director is not working to any set formula or schedule of labour. He may do much, or he may do very little. 'The best play director', said Granville Barker, 'is he who ostensibly does least, not most.' The measure of his task will depend on the play itself—on the degree of interpretation required to make it living to a modern audience. For instance, a Greek play presented in a Victorian theatre building requires a greater degree of interpretation by the director than does *Seagulls over Sorrento*. But to account for the arrival on the scene of the director, we must examine briefly against their background the work of those artists whose influence has done most to establish the balanced relationship which should exist between the various components of the theatre.

The essential components of the theatre are the author and the actor, yet it is to be regretted that these two individuals, whose collaboration is indispensable to the performance of a play, are almost inevitably involved in a struggle for supremacy. The author's centre of interest lies in the total effect of his play on the audience, but, if he is not of the theatre himself, as were Shakespeare, Molière and Wagner, he often lacks the sense of theatrical values that the actor possesses; and, unwilling to admit his shortcomings, resents the actor's attempts to

6

impose theatricalism upon him. Whereas the actor, however sympathetic he may be to the author's play, tends by the necessity of his profession to concern himself principally with his own part in it.

The struggle for supremacy between actor and author was not keenly felt in England until the middle of the 18th century. I believe one reason for the comparative harmony between actor and author during the early part of our dramatic history was due to the actor's need for plays, which made him dependent on the author, and this resulted in a sort of coalition government. The Elizabethan theatre, having no large store of suitable plays, was bound to foster authorship. This need for plays led to a working partnership between Shakespeare and Burbage, Alleyn and Marlowe, and the important influence and prolific work of Jonson, Webster, Dekker, Greene, Beaumont, Fletcher, Ford, Marston and Massinger. The Restoration stage, which substituted the Italian theatre form for the native Elizabethan, was equally hungry for plays written in a suitable style, and again the power of the author balanced that of the actor. But by the middle of the 18th century a sufficiently large repertoire of plays had been built up to allow the actor to pick and choose his acting material according to his personal requirements. As a result there came into existence a new all-powerful leader in the form of the actor-manager. This magnate had it in his power to dispense with the living playwright and to alter and adapt the works of the dead. So that, if the living author was unable or unwilling to write the sort of play which fed the particular requirements of the leading actor, he was unlikely to see his plays performed, for there was an ample storehouse of drama which the actor could adapt to suit his personal needs.

For a period of over a hundred years the author of talent almost disappeared from our stage, whilst the actor-manager gorged himself on the classics, suitably adapted to emphasise the importance of his own role, or presented works of inferior quality, relying solely on his individual talents as an actor to create entertainment. But whether he chose the classics or relied on inferior contemporary material, the actor-manager's choice was conditioned by the suitability of the plays for the display of his personal talents.

At this point I must be careful not to seem to misrepresent the case against the actor. It is no fault in the actor that he chooses only those plays which are suitable for his own performance, though he is often unaware of the range and adaptability of his personal gifts. The fault during the period under discussion lay in the lack of balance between author and actor. Only when a determined author, like Sheridan, fought his way into the actor's theatre was that balance restored for a brief moment. The actor must always choose plays in which he can act well; and it is the author's business to supply plays which can be well acted; but if the actor has a complete monopoly of power the composite Art of the Theatre is unlikely to thrive.

Too great a power in the hands of the actor will lead to sterility. The great actor-managers tended to concentrate on a small repertoire of tragic and melodramatic plays which were frequently repeated, or upon comedies which tended to repeat a certain type of character—the Lord Foppingtons and the Lord Ogilvies on the one hand and the Sir Harry Wildairs and Mr. Horners on the other. This restriction of repertoire led not only to sterility in the writing, but to sterility in acting, which developed little, so far as poetic acting was concerned, from the picturesque style popularised by Edmund Kean and followed by Mathews, Philips, Macready, Irving, Tree, Booth and Martin-Harvey—a style which is still traceable in the so-called 'ham' acting of to-day.

The predominance of the actor-manager over the dramatist was further strengthened by the restriction placed on the building of theatres both in London and in the provinces. From 1737 to 1843, which roughly represents the period during which the dramatist slowly died out, there were only two playhouses licensed for plays in London—Drury Lane and Covent Garden —whereas in Elizabethan times there were at one time as many as fourteen. This limitation of theatres meant that the dramatist had a restricted market for his plays. It was a case of the number of shops being reduced from fourteen to two, and the shop-keepers, thereby, establishing a virtual monopoly of goods which they were prepared to sell. Under such circumstances the manufacturer was no longer in a position to influence the public taste. This restriction of theatres was brought about by necessity. The Puritan Commonwealth had virtually killed the popular taste for drama, and in consequence the Restoration theatre was an esoteric entertainment, almost entirely confined to the Court. But as the influence of Puritanism began to wane, the popularity of the theatre was restored. Instead of building more theatres to meet the increased demand, which would have resulted in more plays and players, the actor-managers, by virtue of the law, merely increased the size of their theatres. As a result Drury Lane and Covent Garden were reconstructed to seat over three thousand spectators, and became suitable only for spectacular productions. The small-scale comedy of manners, so favoured by the Restoration dramatists, or even the classical play in the manner of Racine, became absurd in such vast amphitheatres. Bombast, rhetoric and large-scale spectacle were the only possible mediums of expression. The little plays either disappeared or were treated as prologues or after-pieces to some gigantic spectacle of a naval engagement or a battle with the Turks. We find a satire on this state of affairs in Sheridan's farce of *The Critic*.

To be forced to collaborate in such nonsense, or to be relegated to the position of a soup or a savoury, was yet a further reason why the writers of quality withdrew from the theatre. When, in the middle of the 19th century, the restriction on theatre building was lifted, the habit of partnership between the writer of talent and the actor was broken. The writer of talent had found other markets for his goods, and the actor-manager looked elsewhere for stocking up his new theatres. Busied with the management of their houses and the arduous task of performing leading parts, the actor-managers had little time to devote to the study of the composite Art of the Theatre; their efforts were concentrated on finding vehicles suitable for their own individual talents, and their theatres became show houses for displays of virtuoso performances. In choosing their texts they relied on revivals or plays that followed a proved formula of acceptable entertainment. For comedy and domestic plays they turned to the school of Scribe and Sardou and their English imitators, who provided them with the so-called well-made plays, which—whatever their merits as popular entertainment—were imitative and monotonous in plot and characterisation. For tragedy and melodrama they repeated the well-tried favourites, such as *Richard III* and *Othello*, *A New Way to Pay Old Debts*, *The Lyons Mail*, *The Corsican Brothers*, *The Bells* and *The Wandering Jew*. Little time or care could be given to composite staging or balanced performances. Plays were either mounted with the stock scenery of the playhouse; or, if novelty was required, the business of staging the play was left to men of inferior quality. The doors of the theatre were opened to the sensational showmen who supplied waterfalls, flying fairies, chariot races and erupting volcanoes with little regard to the needs of the play or the artistic values of the theatre. Sensational tricks and poverty of quality, both in play material and in play presentation, degraded the public taste, and the theatre in general lost all pretensions to being a serious intellectual or cultural pursuit. There were some notable exceptions; neither Garrick, Macready nor Irving were cheap showmen, but even the latter, though he displayed a considerable reverence for Shakespeare's texts, was forced by the depraved taste of his age to elaborate his productions to a point where the play was smothered under the scenery and supers.

Take for example this contemporary description of Capulet's feast in his production of *Romeo and Juliet*:

'The gaudy peacocks, just removed from the banquet table, the minstrel's gallery crowded with musicians, the sedila of blue and silver, on which sat the black-haired, pale-faced Rosaline, the trees of azalea, the overhanging drapery of silver brocade, the pages, and the dancers, so distracted the attention that the play was for the moment lost. It seemed impossible to get action with all this magnificence. The play was forced to stop, whilst the eye travelled from one detail to another.'

Yet Irving, for all his elaboration, which at times may have distorted or overloaded the play, was an artist of the theatre, and despite his attachment to the actor-manager's tradition and his biased opposition to the new school of play-writing and production which was growing up under his feet, he did more than any other stage artist of the second half of the 19th century to bring dignity and artistry back to the theatre. We may deplore his lack of taste in his choice of plays, his reliance on spectacle and his over-emphasis on star performance, but we must recognise that he was not only a great actor, but also a great director. His productions were controlled, his actors disciplined, his craftsmanship and planning superb. Above all, he had the singleness of vision which distinguishes all artists. How great his work might have been if he had been able to devote all his energy to production alone and not weakened his vision of the composite work of the theatre by his desire to emphasise his own performance, we can only imagine. For this struggle between the composite Art of the Theatre and the individual art of the actor is the fundamental weakness of the actor-manager's position. The essential egoism of the actor is too often incapable of achieving the just balancing of the theatre's components which makes the theatre a complete art form. Even when the leading actor is able to adjust his mentality correctly, the arduous exigencies of play-acting and play-directing are often too great for one man to undertake without loss to the one or the other. The failure, then, of the actor-managers' theatre, of which Irving was probably the finest product, was due to the fact that too much power was placed in the hands of the actor, who, concentrating as he must on his own art, is generally incapable of promoting the artistry of the whole.

The period of the all-powerful actor-manager which effectively ended with Tree, but still lingers on to-day in the work of Donald Wolfit, is related in feeling to the literary romantic movement. Like all theatre movements, it took an unconscionable time in dying. It is significant that, even outside England, the era of stage romanticism was associated rather with the actors than with the authors. It is true that in Germany romanticism produced such dramatists as Goethe, Schiller and Wagner, but the German theatre was almost devoid of a national repertory before the Sturm und Drang movement. As dramatists, Goethe and Schiller were collaborating with the actors in stocking up the shop, in much the same way as Shakespeare, Jonson, Marlowe and Congreve had stocked up the English repertoire. In France there were Victor Hugo and Alexandre Dumas the Elder; but on the whole it is the names of the actors that we associate with the romantic movement in the theatre—Edmund Kean, Macready, Irving and Tree in England; Ludwig Devrient in Germany; Frédéric Lemaitre in France; Salvini in Italy; Forrest and Booth in America.

Eventually the pressure of the literary realistic movement began to force its way into the last stronghold of romanticism —the theatre. The path had been paved already by the well-made play which, as developed by Wilde and Pinero, took on a social importance, enlarging its significance and quality. Realistic plays were first given by small independent theatres and stage societies. The new plays of Ibsen, Robertson, the Manchester school and eventually of Galsworthy and Shaw found a growing public. Henry James, Shaw and Archer, as dramatic critics, offered battle to the Leviathan of Irving, and although the Leviathan steadfastly refused to listen to Shaw's criticism or to produce his plays, a determined challenge had been made to the might of the actor-managers.

But a revolution powerful enough to overthrow the actor had to come from inside the theatre, rather than from outside it. It was not only new writing that was required, but a new aesthetic of the stage, an aesthetic which included acting, scenic decoration, costume, lighting, and above all a co-ordination of all these elements by a single vision. However brilliant the ideas of the critics or the works of the new authors might be, it was only possible for a man of the theatre to bring about the necessary reform.

Ironically enough this man of the theatre, Edward Gordon Craig, was the son of Irving's leading lady, Ellen Terry, and sprang from the heart of Irving's own company of which he was a member from 1889-97. Ironically, too, Craig never rose to be a leading practitioner of theatre himself, and has often been considered an eccentric and an impractical idealist. To some extent it is true that many of Craig's projects for scenic design—for it is principally through his scenic art that he has spread his gospel—are impractical for any theatre that exists at the moment; but since no manager would entrust Craig with a theatre to work in, he was forced to create a theatre in his own imagination. It is also true that Craig's demands of the theatre are sometimes exaggerated, but Craig was fighting to rescue the theatre from the showman; and if his ideas even now seem ahead of their time, how much more so must they have appeared to his contemporaries. His importance lies in the influence he has shed over the theatre, not only in Great Britain, but in Europe and America.

Craig was, and still is, a man of ideas, a poet of the stage, a dreamer of great dreams, rather than a practising director. His stage productions in London were few. They were neither seen by large audiences, nor did they have any immediate effect on the British theatre. Purcell's *Dido and Æneas* was performed at Hampstead in 1900 and was followed by *The Masque of Love* at the Coronet Theatre, Notting Hill Gate, and Handel's *Acis and Galatea* at the Great Queen Street Theatre. All these operas were produced in collaboration with the composer Martin Shaw. There followed a production of Laurence Housman's *Bethlehem* at the Imperial Institute, South Kensington, and in 1903 he produced *The Vikings of Helgeland* and *Much Ado About Nothing* for Ellen Terry at the Imperial Theatre. That was the total of his work in this country.

Those who saw these productions were amazed at the simplicity—almost severity—of their decoration. Gone were the old wings and borders and painted backcloths. Craig gained his effects by a combination of space and proportion, by a comprehensive colour scheme, expressed in scenery, costumes and lighting. Footlights were dismissed or reduced to a minimum and their place was taken by shafts of light which gave the simple elements of his scenery a sculptural, three-dimensional form. His whole stage was a combination of skilfully blended tones in place of the elaborate, gaudy colours of the contemporary theatre. In *The Vikings* he used dresses of light shades of grey, contrasted with huge semi-circular cloaks of clear and glowing colour. W. B. Yeats in his *Ideas of Good and Evil* writes of 'Gordon Craig's purple backcloth, that made Dido and Æneas seem wandering on the edge of eternity.' The *Times* critic spoke of the impressive effect of his simple, severe scenery—'harmonious in colouring, broad and massive in design.' Craig's work was from the point of view of his time completely original. He turned his back on realism and on the popular concern with archaelogical exactitude. He showed that the theatre was not a branch of an arts and crafts museum, nor a booth for the display of the showman's tricks. But his sweeping reforms were severely cold-shouldered by his countrymen. Craig was offered no opportunities to develop his work in London, and in 1904 he accepted an invitation

14

from Otto Brahm to go to Berlin and produce Otway's *Venice Preserved*. From then onwards his renown on the Continent began to grow, and in 1905 he published 'The Art of the Theatre' in which he formulated his ideas on the type of theatre he wished to see. In this booklet we see an example of Craig's somewhat despotic views of the director's relation to the actor; views for which he was to be bitterly attacked when he wrote an article on 'The Actor and the Uber-Marionette'. Here, in dialogue form between a director and a playgoer, Craig emphasises the task of the artistic director:

STAGE-DIRECTOR: . . If the stage-director was to technically train himself for his task of interpreting the plays of the dramatist—in time, and by a gradual development, he would again recover the ground lost to the theatre, and finally would restore the Art of the Theatre to its home by means of his own creative genius.

PLAYGOER: Then you place the stage-director before the actors?

STAGE-DIRECTOR: Yes; the relation of the stage-director to the actor is precisely the same as that of the conductor to his orchestra, or of the publisher to his printer.

But although it might appear from this and later utterance that Craig regards the actor as a marionette, this is, in fact, far from his philosophy. Craig was himself a distinguished actor; his admiration for, and interest in, actors is unbounded. When Olivier played *Lear* in Paris, Craig was content to sit amongst the instruments in the orchestra pit to witness his performance. I have seen him, as an old man of over seventy, scanning photographs of our contemporary actors with a magnifying glass, as he endeavours to keep himself informed of their qualities and characteristics. I have heard him speak with deep reverence of the acting of Irving and many of his contemporaries. We must not forget that when Craig wrote his fulminations against actors, he was stating the case against the all-powerful position of the actor, as the arbiter of the Art of the

Theatre. What Craig demanded was twofold; first, an aesthetic of theatre—a return to the Art of the Theatre, and secondly, the predominance of an artist director—the unity of production under one man.

A director is not an inventor. There was nothing positively new about Craig's work, but rather a new way of looking at old, forgotten things, and yet when we put a design by Craig beside the vast scenic concoctions of the 19th century, the purity of his style and the clarity of his vision seem as novel and revolutionary as a jet aeroplane set against a zeppelin. Craig reaffirmed the eternal truths of art and called the theatre back to the purity of its origins. His scenic art is a renaissance of the spirit which animated the dignity and grandeur of the Greek theatre, the rhythms of the dance-drama of Bali, the simple truths of the mediaeval and Japanese theatres. He tore away the tinsel, the pretence and the falsity which bad taste had imposed upon the stage. He recognised that, in order to free the theatre from commercial degradation into which it was in danger of falling, and restore it to its position as an art, it was necessary to lift it above the whims of financial promoters and the personal ambitions of actor-managers who, whilst nourishing the art of the actor, had neglected the Art of the Theatre.

Craig was not the first director; there had been others before him. The famous company of the Duke of Saxe-Meinigen had employed an independent director, and the disciplined acting and co-ordination that resulted were generally admired on the Continent. The masters of the Miracle plays were play directors and there have been other spasmodic examples of production as a separate craft throughout the theatre's history, but the introduction of an independent craftsman to organise the business of the stage was usually connected with the larger spectacles such as the Court Masques of James I, and the opera-ballets of Versailles. Craig was the first to champion the cause of the independent artist-director for all plays, and to call for his employment, as being the only effective way of restoring to the theatre the unity which is required by a work of art and which had largely been lost.

Craig's theme was taken up by Oscar Wilde. Deploring the lack of co-ordination in the staging of contemporary plays, Wilde wrote:

'The facts of art are diverse, but the essence of artistic effect is unity. Monarchy, Anarchy and Republicanism may contend for the government of nations; but a theatre should be in the power of a cultured despot. There may be division of labour, but there must be no division of mind. . . . In fact, in art there is no specialism, and a really artistic production should bear the impress of one master, and one master only, who not only should design and arrange everything, but should have complete control over the way in which each dress is to be worn.'

Craig's challenge to the existing state of affairs in the British theatre was to meet with no immediate response. The vested interests of the actor-managers and the commercial promoters of popular theatre were too strong to be speedily moved from their strongholds by the impassioned appeal of an artist. But if people in England were slow to receive his ideas, those abroad were not. He travelled widely on the Continent, where he discovered a sympathetic movement in the process of growth, influenced by the work of Adolph Appia and Stanislavsky. Craig both influenced this new movement and absorbed what it had to tell him. His thoughts were expressed in a periodical which he edited, called 'The Mask', and in his brilliant woodcuts and drawings. It was all a part of the growing desire for a change in the ways of the theatre as it had existed in the 19th century. Perhaps the person who was the most effective exponent of Craig's theories was Max Reinhardt who, being a more practical workman and a better propagandist than Craig, was able to exploit his theories, influencing the whole

2   17

German-speaking stage. Reinhardt reaped much of the honour and profit that should have come to our own British maestro.

Craig, however, remained and still remains an exile from his native land. British theatrical managers have not been prepared to risk their money, nor been prepared to show the forbearance necessary to allow him to undertake a production. The only major productions that Craig accomplished since his departure from London in 1904 were *Venice Preserved* for the Lessing Theatre in Berlin, *Hamlet* for Stanislavsky at the Moscow Arts Theatre in 1912, and Ibsen's *The Pretenders* for the Royal Theatre, Copenhagen, in 1926. It is both strange and ironic that our greatest theatrical artist, whose ideas have been followed, developed and exploited, should to-day be living on the charity of his friends.

Meanwhile the ideas that Craig let loose on the Continent were slowly returning to percolate the stronghold of the British 19th-century traditionalists; and his arguments for the leadership of an independent director were strengthened by the work of another man of the theatre in the person of Harley Granville Barker. In many ways Barker represented a diametrically opposite approach to the theatre to Craig. The latter stressed the independence of the Art of the Theatre both from the art of acting and the art of play-writing, whereas Barker was intent on insuring firstly the author's rights in the theatre, and secondly on showing the actor how he could benefit from a true understanding of the play as a whole.

As a director Barker was largely influenced by the realistic movement that was growing up around him. Himself a considerable playwright of the realistic school, he was drawn towards the plays of Ibsen, Shaw and Galsworthy, and the constructive criticism of the younger-minded critics such as Archer, Grein and Shaw. More fortunate than Gordon Craig, he was able to secure a lease of the Court Theatre in 1903 which he opened with six matinées of *Candida*. There was little money at the disposal of the courageous Vedrenne-Barker management, but, as the events showed, there were unlimited possibilities in the form of a new dramatic literature. The policy of this management was not to make money by extended runs of a few plays, but to cram as many first-rate plays as possible into the repertoire. As the tale of a memorable series of first nights unfolded, it became apparent that a new school of acting and production was coming into being under the leadership of a director of genius. If Craig represented the new school of poetic production, Barker was the first great British realistic director. Yet his productions were not confined to realistic plays; his greatest successes were achieved in three memorable Shakespearean revivals at the Savoy Theatre, starting in 1912— *A Winter's Tale*, *A Midsummer Night's Dream*, and *Twelfth Night*. With a brilliantly balanced company led by Henry Ainley, he allied the virile traditions of English Shakespearean acting to the clear thought and imaginative pungency of Shaw's critical writing. Sweeping away the over-loaded scenic devices of Sir Herbert Beerbohm Tree, he substituted his own carefully studied knowledge of Shakespeare's aims and intentions. His approach to the theatre might be called a literary approach, and he himself should be regarded as one of the first of the school of theatrical scholar-directors—a school that has been continued by Coghill, Rylands and Wilson Knight. In the 16th and 17th centuries it was not unusual for actors and playwrights to be University men, but in the 18th and 19th centuries acting and scholarship did not often go together. The University of the Crummles family was centred round the theatrical hamper, their pens were sticks of grease-paint; their studies confined to 'getting up' their parts. To-day we have almost reached a position where a University degree coupled with a gold medal from a dramatic academy are essential requisites for a theatrical director.

Barker, like Craig, is better known by his writings than his productions. His Shakespeare prefaces with their careful analyses of plot and character are a model of how a producer should approach his text. They reveal Barker's scholarship and literary taste, qualities not shared to any marked degree by Craig. Craig, in his anxiety to rescue the Art of the Theatre from the untheatricality of the author on the one hand and the over-theatricality of the actor on the other, declared, 'We shall no longer need the assistance of the playwrights', but such remarks by Craig should not be taken too literally; he was fighting for his Art of the Theatre and he was anxious to show that this art was greater than that of the author or the actor. Barker, by placing emphasis on the inter-relation of author, actor and director, restored the balance.

Yet another undermining influence was to weaken the actor-manager's methods of staging a play. In the years immediately preceding the 1914–18 war, an amateur, William Poel, attracted the attention of the connoisseurs by presenting Shakespearean and other pre-Restoration plays with a simplicity which exposed the full extent of the actor's digression. The giant spectacles of the actor-managers with their reliance on realistic effects and archaeological details, such as a spurious mime of John signing Magna Carta in *King John*, real rabbits in *A Midsummer Night's Dream* and a herd of deer in *As You Like It*, had smothered Shakespeare beneath a pile of scenery, and the actor-manager beneath a pile of bills. Poel with a small band of enthusiasts presented Shakespeare's plays in simple halls, hired for the occasion, making use of a platform stage similar in form to the Elizabethan. The actors were taught to speak rapidly and clearly and dispense with elaborate scenery, rhetoric and vocal tricks. Continuity of action was restored to the plays, in place of the elaborate scenic divisions of the Italian theatre tradition. Although only a small public was privileged to see these revelations, the effect on the acting profession was profound. Poel not only influenced Barker, but his direct influence can be traced in the work of Nugent Monck at the Maddermarket Theatre, Norwich, and in the modern trend towards the platform stage of neo-Elizabethan directors.

The influence of Craig, Poel and Barker established the importance of the director as the co-ordinator and leader of stage production in this country. But an even stronger influence was to come from abroad through the Moscow Arts Theatre. Constantin Stanislavsky was principally an actor, and his message was first addressed to his fellow players. He called for team acting, as against virtuoso performances. He laid down a method of training the actor which shook the whole philo-sophy of the Crummles' school of intuition and bombast. He demanded truth of interpretation; and this he claimed can be attained only by rigorous discipline, both mental and physical, by perfection of technique, by ceaseless self-criticism, and by the absorption of the actor in the life and philosophy of the character he is studying. As a director Stanislavsky believed that the way to achieve the Art of the Theatre lay in working through the actors. To this extent he differed from Craig, who held that the artist-director is more important than the players. Stanislavsky was prepared to explain and discuss his methods with his actors. He was open to their criticism and welcomed their ideas, believing that, if the actors are working to a recognised method, they are themselves capable of creating the Art of the Theatre. Craig, the poetic visionary on his lonely heights, demanded absolute obedience to the captain of the ship who alone could steer it to the mystical realms of theatrical art.

The full influence of Stanislavsky did not reach England until his books were translated in the late 1930's, but many of his ideas and much of his method was transmitted to our stage through the work of Kommisarjevsky. Meanwhile, the new school of stage production influenced by Stanislavsky, Rein-hardt and Craig was gaining ground abroad, led by Jessner and Piscator in Germany; Antoine, Pitoef, Gaston Baty and Jouvet in France; Norman Bel Geddes and Lee Simonson in America.

I am aware that in reeling off this list of names I have omitted many that have better and more enduring claims to fame, but in the theatre the past is so soon over, and the present so hard to judge. There is one other, however, who would make more claim on our attention were he not divided from us by an Iron Curtain—not of theatrical design. I believe his work is likely to have some influence upon the future—I refer to Bertolt Brecht. In his method of rehearsal Brecht has followed closely the precepts of Stanislavsky. But his philosophy of the theatre, which he calls Epic Theatre, is new or rather a renaissance of a past theatrical stream which does not stem directly from the illusionist theatre. Epic Theatre is the antithesis of the theatre of illusion and make-belief. The theatre, Brecht believes, should not try to deceive the spectator by drawing him into the simulated emotions of the players. The players must represent the emotions whilst keeping the spectator alive to the wider implications of the author's purpose.

In the Greek theatre the audience was conscious that the grotesquely masked figures on the stage were actors miming certain emotions; they were not under the impression that the actors were actually experiencing those emotions. We find a similar process in the Japanese theatre where certain stylised expressions and gestures represent joy and sorrow. This tradition was found to some extent in the acting of the Commedia dell' Arte. In the illusionist theatre the actor's art is to conceal his art; he makes you believe he is happy or unhappy, clever or stupid, honest or false. In Brecht's Epic Theatre the actor uses his art to indicate emotions as an illustration of the play's theme.

In his own finest play, *Mother Courage*, Brecht interleaves the action with songs. The play depicts the story of a vivandière following her trade of selling goods to the troops during the Thirty Years' War; and the action relates how she loses all her children during this seemingly endless struggle. The moral that Brecht wants us to see is that those who live by war must also contribute to war. Mother Courage has to pay for her livelihood with her sons. The songs paint this moral, and also portray the suffering and courage of the pawns of war. These songs are treated as a sort of Greek chorus or comment on the situation. The characters step forward from the play, shattering the illusion of reality, to point the play's message. It is not unlike the operetta technique applied to drama, only in the operetta the didactic songs are about love or how we should all be gay, on such a beautiful day.

Brecht's attempt to break with the technique of deception and illusion is, I think, a salutary medicine for the theatre in an age when the films and television can do these things so much better, but to impose a didactic purpose on a play is dangerous. 'The author's text', says Brecht, 'is only sacred in so far as it is true.' We are bound to ask what he means by truth—is it theatrical truth or political truth? Unfortunately that word has so many meanings.

In the work of Craig, Barker and Stanislavsky, we see the fundamental principles of modern production emerging, and the emphasis being laid on the existence of the theatre as an art, inside which the author and the actor have their contributions to make. Gradually the tradition of the actor-manager began to crumble, broken down no less by the heavy costs of the mammoth spectacles, than by the ridicule which a public, enlightened by intelligent criticism, began to heap upon it. With the fall of the great actor-managers, the authors again entered the theatre and the 19th century ushered in Ibsen, Wilde, Pinero, Tchechov, Strindberg and Maeterlinck, Shaw, Yeats, Barry, Synge, Galsworthy, O'Neill and Hauptmann. A new age of playwrights had dawned, and in its wake came the director as an established fact.

The plays these new authors wrote could no longer be supported only by the virtuoso performances of the actor-managers, they required the new aesthetic of the stage that Craig had preached and Stanislavsky had carried out. So whilst Poel and the prefaces of Barker had prepared the ground for the advent of the director for Shakespeare, the new dramatists supported the case of the director for contemporary drama, if for no better reason than to safeguard their work from the ravages of the all-powerful actor-managers.

But even if the actor-manager has all but disappeared from our contemporary stage, the box-office is still largely controlled by the star actors. It is no use bemoaning the star system, it is folly to ignore it. We may deplore the depravity of Hollywood journalism, but it is, after all, only an extension of a demand which is inherent in all dramatic life. I have no doubt the Greek theatre had its stars, and so did the Roman; Burbage was a star and Betterton, and, I am sure, Nell Gwynne was as satisfactory to her publicity agent as is Rita Hayworth. The theatre lives and benefits by the personalities of its leading players. They have, and always will have, a greater reality for the public than the authors or directors. Nor should it be imagined that actor-worship is confined to the degenerate capitals and film studios. The provincial repertories have their stars and cultivate them.

This hold that the actor has on the affection of the public places a power in his hands which can be, and often is, a disadvantage to the public, the author and himself. To the public because it can limit the plays to those suitable to the personality of the leading actor; to the author because it results in the system of long-runs, which may benefit the lucky few, but does not encourage the many; to the actor because, like all power, if used to excess, it corrupts. The balance of nature which requires a greater equilibrium for a state than can be achieved by the rule of one man has, therefore, invented the director and pitched him, kicking and protesting, into the middle of the fray, not only to hold the balance, but to insure that the Art of the Theatre can live.

There is, however, a danger inherent in the system of the all-powerful director, no less than in that of the all-powerful actor. This new potentate can as easily fall a victim to the corruption of power as can the star actor. In Russia, no sooner had the director won his battle over the romantic actors, than he began to exploit his triumph by indulging in every form of idio-syncrasy in the pretence and, perhaps, in the belief, that this was creative vision. The movement of strange and exotic pro-duction was seen in the work of Tairov and Meyerhold and those gymnastic displays on parallel bars which were called Constructivism.

The director, unrestrained and raised to the level of a god, can chase the author once more from the stage and reduce the actor to a puppet. Extremist production has, however, found little root in Britain, though examples of it were found at the Cambridge Festival Theatre—and in some of Kommisar-jevsky's productions of Shakespeare. For this rejection of extremism there are two main reasons: one—the obvious one—is the conventionality of the British public which clings to traditional progress in the theatre as in other walks of life. The second, and more potent reason, is that the British theatre is mainly controlled by a balance of power between manager, director and leading actor, and although the director is now recognised as the arbiter of the play's style he is, for better or worse, dependent on getting his views accepted by manager and star players. Under this form of restraint he is unlikely to indulge in the more exotic forms of production.

As a result, the general tendency of British production to-day is conservative. The full implications of Craig's artistic dictatorship have not been accepted; although his principle of unified co-ordination under the director has. This conservative tendency leads to a certain lack of progressive development in the British method of staging a play, which remains more sober and less exciting than in Russia or Germany. On the other hand, it may be claimed that it favours an equitable balance between the actor and the author who are, after all, the basic elements on which good theatre must be founded.

My predecessor* in giving these lectures referred to the strange practice of the theatre in resisting and finally banishing 'the artist whom it considers austere, or too original, or too uncompromising'. I do not think this practice is confined to the theatre; it is true of other walks of life and there are notable examples in the Bible. In other arts, however, this practice is not so final; for, although the painter who is ahead of his time—and what great painter was not?—may gain recognition when he is dead, the actor and the director must either gain an audience during their working life or be confined to the dustbin of oblivion. This time restriction which is placed on the artist in the theatre, though severe, is a challenge. The actor or director who fails to impress the audience of to-day can make no claim on the audience a hundred years hence. The impression must be made now, and to a great extent in terms of the conditions as they now exist; for, however pressing the desire for reform may be—be it in the sphere of stage architecture, design, methods of acting, or production—the theatrical artist must, if he wants to succeed, measure his activities against the ephemeral conditions in which he works. It may be tragic that Craig, Kommisarjevsky, St. Denis, Granville Barker and other more talented directors were either rejected or resigned in despair from the English theatre, but no director, be he genius or nonentity, can escape from the law of the stage:

'The drama's laws the drama's patrons give
And we, who seek to please, must please to live.'

I have said that Craig and Barker exerted a greater influence through their writing than through their productions. This must be our consolation for their loss. The memory of the actor when he acts, or the director when he directs, is confined

* Michael Redgrave in 'The Actor's Ways and Means' (Heinemann).

26

to the memory of those who saw his work. He who desires to reform the stage would be wise to find more permanent ways than the stage can offer to do so. If he chooses the stage as his platform, he must succeed in making his point within the little—the very little—span of time that is granted him.

In pleading for the cause of the Art of the Theatre I am no high-brow. I do not believe that the Art of the Theatre exists only when the play is by Shakespeare or Goethe and the acting by Gielgud or Werner Krauss. The theatre is the most popular of all the arts. Not only must it be understandable to all the people—or at least to all the people who are capable of understanding—but it can, and should, more often make use of the simplest and most popular material. There is nothing to prevent *Oklahoma* or *Jack the Giant Killer* from being transformed into works of art, but there must be—besides superb craftsmanship—both a unifying vision and theatrical truth; there must be a soul as well as a body.

I said earlier in this lecture that when we leave the theatre inspired and elevated, not merely by the author and actor, but by the existence of the theatre itself, we can say we have witnessed the Art of the Theatre. I would like now to redraft that definition by saying that when we leave the theatre unaware of the separate existence of author, actor or director, but aware only of the existence of that illuminating experience we call the theatre, then, and only then, can we say we have witnessed the Art of the Theatre. Unfortunately the state of affairs which forces the theatre to be an industry, rather than an art, makes it difficult for directors, managers, authors, actors and designers in this country to maintain those high principles of their calling which can transform the theatre into an art.

I am not optimistic enough to imagine that all theatre can be an art, but I am demanding enough to state that the director's task is to try to make it so. The showman with few exceptions is not interested in art; he hides behind the catchword of entertainment. The actor, unless he is nourished in Stanislavsky's nursery, is too busy seeking personal success. The author is seldom an experienced technician in matters of stage production. Only the director remains to safeguard the Art of the Theatre. For this he was created, and this is his trust;- if he fails to fulfil it, his function is useless.

The Director and the Author

'THE most desirable director of a play', said Shaw, 'is the author.' Yet how few authors of to-day are able to instil life into the production of their own plays or, indeed, are willing to spend time and labour pursuing the craftsmanship of the stage. In my first lecture I reminded you of the close connexion between author and actor in the process of building our native theatre, and how, once the theatre was plentifully stocked with plays, the author of quality all but disappeared, both as a writer of plays and as a member of the stage team. Although since the beginning of this century good plays are again in demand and the author of quality can now count on the stage absorbing all the good plays he can write, the habit of the author-technician has largely ceased to exist. There are, of course, exceptions. There are authors who are directors and authors who are actors, but it is generally true that the contemporary author, like the Victorian parent, commands our respect and sometimes our awe, but is not expected to soil his hands by bathing the children.

Shaw explains the temperamental aloofness of the author from the drudgery of rehearsals as follows:

'Unfortunately, as play-writing is a solitary occupation which gives no social training, some playwrights are so lacking in

29

the infinite patience, intense vigilance, consideration for others, and imperturbable good manners which directing requires, that their presence at rehearsals is a hindrance instead of a help.'

It is, perhaps, only natural that an author who has finally laid down his pen after many months, or even years, of imaginative effort, creating and mentally co-habiting with his characters, should be sometimes, though not always, temperamentally unsuited to help the actors through the painful birth-pangs of creating those characters all over again, and doing so by a method which is fundamentally different from that of the author.

Ibsen either drew his characters from life, or if they were purely imaginary, asserted that he saw and was visited by them. In the case of Nora in *A Doll's House*, he described her exact appearance as she leant over his shoulder. Indeed, most authors, if they do not actually draw their characters from life, create mental pictures of them, and these pictures are, I suspect, far more real and satisfactory than the personalities of the actors who play them.

The author, who is remote from the theatre, is inclined to be suspicious of any further creative process taking place which might develop or sully such personal vision. Yet this further creative process is a necessary part of the actor's art, for the actor is not visited by visions of the character he is to play, nor can he assume a personality provided for him by the author without some measure of adapatation in terms of his own emotional and physical limitations. This does not mean that the actor exploits his own personality at the expense of the author's character, though of course this does happen, but it means that in the creation of character a compromise between author and actor is essential. For this reason there is not one interpretation of Nora in *A Doll's House*, but hundreds.

To Ibsen such a variety of interpretation might come as a

shock. For him Nora was a person he knew and loved, she must look just so, and speak just so, but to the actress playing this part such limitations would result in artifice.

It is not the author's lack of good manners and patience, as Shaw suggests, which sometimes prejudices the actor against allowing the author to direct his performance; it is the actor's fear that an author, who is no longer a member of the stage team, may resent or restrict the actor's creative process—that strange process which consists of merging the actor's character with the character created by the author. This process must take place if the result is to be a living creation, and not just a dead recital of the author's words.

Practical collaboration between author and actor is most effective when the author is writing his play for a specific actor, or for a team of players, as was the case with Marlow, Shakespeare, Jonson, Molière and Congreve. In such cases the playwright is using the characteristics of the actor as he creates the character. And in such cases Shaw's dictum may be right, that the most desirable director of a play is the author.

But apart from temperamental reasons, there are technical reasons why the author has assumed an aloofness from stage work and chosen to delegate the process of interpretation to a director. We must not forget that the staging of a play has not only become infinitely more technical since Shakespeare's day, it has also become more cosmopolitan. Plays are seldom written for one actor or for one company, as they were in the days of the Mediaeval guilds or of Shakespeare and Molière—they are written for the widest possible market. Not only are they reproduced in theatres throughout the length and breadth of our own commonwealth of language, but they are translated and performed in countries as widely different in language and stage technique as Russia and Japan, as well as being performed on the radio, on television, and adapted for the cinema. No author could spare the time to reproduce his play in the many different languages and media in which it may be performed during his lifetime, nor would he be qualified to do so.

The French dramatist and novelist, Henri de Montherlant, has recently announced that he must abandon writing plays, because the business of interviewing agents and managements, discussing theatres, leading actors and directors, rewriting scenes to fit the requirements of the manager or the director, adapting the script for broadcasting and television, checking translations and arranging the text for publication, as well as watching rehearsals and enduring the nervous strain of a first performance, makes too great a demand on an author's time and energy. It is true that an author to-day has to devote far more time to the business of getting his play produced, than he did in the days of the stock companies; the production of a play has become infinitely more complicated, and its ramifications far wider. As a result, being a successful playwright is a full time job with little time to spare to devote to the actual business of rehearsal.

Finally, there is, of course, a more empirical reason why the author cannot be the normal director of his own play—he is probably dead—a condition which actor, designer and stage technician consider most desirable.

The old habit of the author-technician has not, however, completely died out, and the contemporary author seeks to maintain his influence over the stage production by inserting lengthy stage directions. I do not mean the simple, necessary, instructions such as: 'Enter one with a bloudie knife', which is obviously a producer-author's note, but the omnibus production instructions employed by such authors as Pinero, Shaw and Barrie, which are a visualisation of the play in action. Such for example, is this direction concerning Miss Phoebe's behaviour at the ball from *Quality Street*:

'They make much of her, and she purrs naughtily at their stroking, with lightning peeps at Miss Susan. Affronted Providence seeks to pay her out by sending Ensign Blades into the tent. Then the close observer may see Miss Phoebe's heart sink like a bucket in a well . . .'

Or consider the difference between the laconic 'Here they fight' of *Henry VI*, and:

'The air above is suddenly rent with shrieks and the clash of steel. Though they cannot see, the boys know that Hook and his crew are upon the Indians. Mouths open and remain open, all in mute appeal to Peter. He is the only boy on his feet now, a sword in his hand, the same he slew Barbicue with, and in his eye is the lust of battle . . .'

and so on, for a page and a half.

But as well as arranging the actors and instructing them in what expressions their faces shall wear, the contemporary playwright often chooses to paint the scenery and place the furniture as well:

'It is after dinner in January 1906, in the library of Lady Britomart Undershaft's house in Wilton Crescent. A large and comfortable settee is in the middle of the room, upholstered in dark leather. A person sitting on it would have, on his right, Lady Britomart's writing table, with the lady herself at it; a smaller writing table behind him on the left; the door behind him on Lady Britomart's side; and a window with a window-seat directly on his left; near the window is an armchair.'

Even the lighting does not escape the diligent author's attention:

'The last remaining rays of light gather into a white radiance descending on Joan.'

Moreover, to fix even more definitely the form that the play should take, it is customary for an acting-edition of the play

3   33

to be published after its first production, which, besides inform-
ing us at what precise moment the actor shall light a cigarette,
also provides a complete list of properties, diagrams of the
stage lay-out, a lighting plot and a description of the costumes
to be worn. With this omnibus of technical details it would
seem that the author, far from remaining aloof from the stage
work, may claim to be an absolute dictator of it. But by seeking
to control the play from outside the theatre, instead of inside
it, the author is in danger of preventing it from breathing at all.
The text of a play cannot be submitted to the crystallising
process of a novel; it must be capable of interpretation and its
interpretation must depend on the conditions of the age in
which it is performed, on the customs and language of the
audience, and last, but not least, on that essential and variable
human factor, the temperament and personalities of the actors
who are to perform it.

I do not want you to think that I am condemning the author
who writes elaborate stage directions; they can be a delightful
commentary to the reader and a help to the director, indicating
the lines along which the author was thinking. Barrie's stage
directions are wholly enchanting, and I often think should be
read aloud by a commentator at the side of the stage. Moreover,
it is right that the author should visualise the play as a live
performance when he is writing it; and, to do so, he must create
a stage on which it is performed. He must, in fact, produce
and act the play mentally for himself. What is wrong is for
the author to insist that the stage directions which he provides
for his imaginary actors shall be copied exactly by the many
different actors who will perform his play in front of many
different audiences. It is wrong for the director to rely slavishly
on the author's stage directions or on the detailed notes of the
acting edition, for to do so results in imitation, not creation,
and the interpretation of a play must be creative if it is to
live. Both actor, director and designer must interpret such
directions in the light of the specific conditions of their own
performance and expression.

34

If, then, we are to allow the director the liberty of altering the author's stage directions, to what extent is he at liberty to alter the script itself? Shaw is adamant:

'The director, having considered the play, and decided to undertake the job of directing it, has no further concern with its literary merits or its doctrine (if any).'

In general we must agree with him, but there are exceptions; and we must not completely discard Brecht's view that 'the text is only sacred in so far as it is true'. Even experienced playwrights would be foolish not to listen to suggestions from an experienced director, actor or manager, on questions of audience reaction and stage-craft. Such suggestions are unlikely to concern the literary or doctrinal merits of the play—unless there is a danger of the play falling foul of the Lord Chamberlain—for it was precisely these merits which persuaded the director to undertake its production. More commonly the director's suggestions will concern matters of stage-craft, such as cuts in the text, clarification of a passage or providing a few extra lines to cover an exit. If the playwright is a good craftsman, like Shaw, technical suggestions will probably be impertinent. Indeed, Shaw regarded them as such, and allowed no alteration to lines or cuts to be made in his plays during his lifetime; yet neither Eliot nor Tchechov have been too proud to use their directors as their first audience and rely on them to give advice on necessary alterations in the script. Shakespeare's texts give ample evidence of rewriting, which must often have been undertaken at the request of the actor or because of the physical differences between one stage and another. But suggestions are one thing and alterations another. The director must not usurp the author's function by altering the script himself; better to demonstrate the weakness to the author in rehearsal—if he cannot see it himself in the script. Some authors deliberately prefer to leave a scene or an incident in rough form until they have a chance of seeing it in rehearsal.

35

Priestley, for instance, often deliberately over-writes his plays, so as to allow the director a choice of cuts after the play has begun to take shape.

Clearly it is wrong to be too dogmatic about such matters, if both author, director and actor are there to serve the theatre, and if there is trust and humility on all sides, there is no need for rules. If the author is dead, however, there is a temptation to treat his script more arbitrarily, a temptation which the director must endeavour to resist. Cuts for time in Shakespeare, providing these do not seriously damage the literary or story value, may often be necessary, but these should only be undertaken if all other doors are closed. The director should remember that it is better to cut the scene changes than the text.

In the 18th century the actors were faced with a difficulty in the case of Shakespeare's plays. Firstly, because the plays were not written to be played with painted scenery and no management of the time would have dared to present a play without the fashionable adornments of the period; secondly, because in feeling and humour they often appeared coarse and barbaric to the taste of the times. In the circumstances there seem to have been only two practical alternatives: to abandon the plays, or to alter them. Looking back on the history of our drama, we might wish they had abandoned them. Perhaps, as a result, more new plays would have been written. In the event they altered the plays to suit their tastes and the requirements of their stage. To-day we can find very little case for such vandalism as Nahum Tate's happy ending to *King Lear*, or the alterations to the tomb scene in *Romeo and Juliet*, or the flagrant removal of scenes and characters which are inherent in the development of the plays. The recent tendency in Shakespeare production is to play the full text, wherever possible, even though there may be obscurities which the audience do not fully understand; for the stage has come to realise that the plays are far more delicately balanced than was once supposed, and to cut one passage will often destroy the effect of the next.

36

I would not maintain, however, that Shakespeare's text should be treated as sacrosanct; he was a stage-worker himself, and, were he living to-day, he would be unlikely to permit a passage to remain which was incapable of being understood by a contemporary audience. But, before making cuts, the director should be certain that what he is doing is an honest endeavour to serve the play and not a surreptitious method of making the play serve his interpretation.

Let us now come to grips, as far as we can, with this question of what we mean by the director's interpretation. In my first lecture I referred to the soul as apart from the body of a pro-duction—the body being the knowledge and application of stage technique and the soul being the director's vision which causes things to happen the way they do. There is nothing mystical about this act of vision, most of us possess it in some form or another. When we read a book, or a poem, or, some-times, when we hear a piece of music, we conjure up a mental image of the characters, the landscape, the atmosphere, per-haps, of these things. Such mental images are first delineated for us by the writer, but our interpretations of them will be influenced by the things we ourselves have felt or seen, and each one will conjure up his own individual image.

The illustrator of a novel, or a story, performs the same sort of visualisation of a scene or a character as the director; but, whereas the illustrator's vision is carried out by him personally and within the comparatively circumscribed scope of graphic art, the director's vision must extend, not only to the scenery—which, in any case, he probably only indicates to his designer—but to the whole scope of the theatre complex, expressed not by him personally but by actors, designer, composer and tech-nicians. But both the director's vision, and the illustrator's, will be a form of personal expression of the text. It will vary, not only according to the style, temperament, horizon and receptive powers of the interpreter, but also according to the type of audience at which the vision is aimed. *Gulliver's Travels* presented to children will bear a different style of illustration from the same book aimed at adult readers. Probably the most frequently visualised of all stories is the story of the Crucifixion, but whether it be painted by Fra Angelico, Matthias Grunewald, Guido Reni, El Greco or Salvador Dali, the vision of each painter can remain faithful to the Evangelist and at the same time be personal to the painter himself.

The degree of vision that we bring to a play will vary according to the type of the play we are producing. In social or realistic drama, such as Congreve's *The Way of the World*, or Ibsen's *Ghosts*, our vision is strictly confined to a definite period and to a style of acting, scenic decoration, lighting and movement. In poetic drama, such as the Elizabethan and Greek plays or the plays of Yeats and Maeterlinck, the vision will be more variable and more individual. The degree of variation must depend not only on the type of play, but on what we might call the degree of its universality. There will be a greater degree of variable vision in a poetic play like *Hamlet* than in a realistic play like Pinero's *The Second Mrs. Tanqueray*; for the one, though it may have its time and place, has implications which can be extended beyond these frontiers, the other has not. We are not necessarily being disloyal to Shakespeare if we visualise *Hamlet* in modern dress, but we are being disloyal to Pinero if we present his play out of its period and without the social implications that this period imposes upon it.

But the director's vision, though it be a personal interpretation of the author's script, must be more strictly disciplined than that of the casual reader or the illustrator of a story book; for, since the theatre is a composite art, he must take into account the all important contribution of the actors, who are to paint the picture for him, as well as the framework within which his vision is to take its shape. He must arrive at a conception of the play which can be related practically to the stage and auditorium, to the equipment and budget of his production, and above all to the audience who are to be entertained by it.

The relationship between the director and the audience is complementary to the relationship between the director and the author; for to interpret the latter's work with loyalty implies interpreting it to the audience as a living work of art—as something which is within their horizon of experience. Now the audience will vary from age to age and from place to place. To-day the witches of *Macbeth* will tend to cause laughter rather than horror, and what may delight an audience in London may have the reverse effect in New York. If the director seeks to serve the author then he must also seek to please the audience, but the rules of the game are that he must only do so by means of the text which the author has provided. Yet by the laws of contradiction by which the stage is bound, the only sure anchor to which the director can hold in this see-saw of pleasing both author and audience is eventually to please himself. If he tries to please others he will almost certainly fail. The director's integrity and attitude are eventually the only rules that are sound, and all we can do is to indicate what that attitude should be and to demand that there should be complete integrity of outlook.

The further we move away from the play, either in time or space, the greater will be the need for interpretation. A Greek play or a Chinese play will need a greater degree of interpretation to a British audience than a play by Terence Rattigan or Somerset Maugham, and these in turn will require a measure of interpretation to a German or Japanese audience. In Prague some years ago a performance of *The Second Mrs. Tanqueray* was given, in which the servants of Aubrey Tanqueray appeared in hunting pink with top-hats; ridiculous you will say, but I have little doubt that our English production of *Lady Precious Stream* would appear no less ridiculous to a Chinese audience.

The audience at the Globe most probably saw Macbeth raging round the stage dressed in a ruff, pursued by a lusty youth dressed in a farthingale, resembling Mary Queen of Scots; but was Garrick wrong to dress him in knee breeches, or

Betterton to present him in a full-bottomed wig, or Irving to present him in a kilt? Some years ago I was responsible for a production of *Much Ado About Nothing* in Bristol, in which the characters were dressed in a sort of Italian-Sicilian costume. The soldiers, Benedick, Claudio, Don Pedro, were dressed in uniforms resembling those of pre-war Spanish or Italian officers, whilst Don John and his underlings wore the black shirts of Mussolini's hirelings. Hero, Beatrice, and the ladies were dressed in Sicilian style; Dogberry, Verges and the Watch wore air-raid warden's helmets. The play was set in a Sicilian courtyard and the dances were accompanied by Italian folk-music. The production seemed to please those who saw it in Bristol, and won much praise from the critics there; whereas, later in London, the same production was faulted by some critics as being unhelpful to the play. I want to make it quite clear I have not mentioned this disagreement of critics in order to display their inconsistencies, but to illustrate what I am trying to say about the relation between director and author on one side, and director and audience on the other. Looking back on this performance, across the years that allow one's judgement to be formed, I believe it was a reasonable interpretation of the play to the Bristol public of those times. My purpose was to show that Shakespeare's comedy was not a dull subject for the matriculation of schools, but that given the eyes to see, it can have the same romance and wit to-day as it had to the Elizabethans who saw it first. The fact that Don Pedro and his companions were officers returning from a campaign makes them specially romantic to Beatrice and Hero, though Beatrice is anxious to prevent anyone from thinking so. But if we dress them as Elizabethan soldiers, the full impact of that romance is lost, for that costume does not suggest the romance of military adventure to us as strongly as it did to an Elizabethan audience. The civilian watchmen, who are undertaking guard duties, can be equally unfunny to us, unless we can relate them to modern experience, and Dogberry can too easily become either a monster or a bore. The play appealed to me as a romantic story with a sophisticated wit; and I found full expression of this feeling, as well as a way of interpreting this play to an audience who were not wholly converted to Shakespeare, in this vision of the play. The production had, I believe, its effect on the Bristol audience and did something to popularise Shakespeare; the London critics, no doubt, could afford to wonder what it was all about.

The Germans have a useful word—Zeitgeist—which can be best translated as the feeling, or mood, of the times. In the interpretation of a play Zeitgeist plays a double role. Firstly, the play itself, however universal its theme, has a mood or atmosphere which belongs to its epoch. Noel Coward's *Cavalcade* has this Zeitgeist no less than *Hamlet*. Thus, the director must take note of the Zeitgeist in which the play was written, and, often because of which, it took the form it did. Secondly, he must tune his interpretation to the Zeitgeist of his audience. To present *Macbeth* without taking into account its Jacobean-Renaissance mood of profound spiritual upheaval, without understanding the contemporary controversy about the power of witchcraft, without bearing in mind that it was written for a particular kind of theatre, is to be disloyal to the author. But to present the play taking only these historical factors into account is to be equally disloyal, since it places the author outside the horizon of his audience, and thereby denies the performance that degree of common application without which it has no life.

So the director's vision of a play must try to find a formula by which he can convey the author's Zeitgeist to the common experience of the audience of his own country and his own time. We are told that Irving's production of *Hamlet* was a masterpiece in its day; I suspect we would giggle at it now, for Irving's interpretation was in tune with the feeling and mood of his age and that feeling or mood is different from ours. We have only to see the film of the great Sarah Bernhardt acting her role in *La Dame Aux Camellias* to realise how far removed our conventions are from those of fifty years ago.

I have said there will be a greater degree of variation in the interpretation of a play like *Hamlet* than there will be in a play like *The Second Mrs. Tanqueray*. Is not this partly due to the fact that *Hamlet* has come down to us almost without stage directions, whereas *The Second Mrs. Tanqueray* is liberally supplied with such helpful hints as 'sniffing the salts' or 'wistfully sitting at the writing table'? I do not think so. Even if the original prompt copy of *Hamlet* was discovered to-morrow, complete with full instructions as to how the Ghost was to vanish and what frock Ophelia was to wear, I should still maintain that the contemporary director would be right to visualise the play for himself, helpful and fascinating as he might find the author's notes, for Shakespeare's notes would apply to an age and a stage-craft which no longer has any reality to the common experience of our audience. The reason why our vision of Hamlet will be more open to variation than our vision of Mrs. Tanqueray is partly that our audience is closer in time to the Zeitgeist of Pinero, and partly because the range and universality of Hamlet is greater than that of Mrs. Tanqueray. The greater the play, then, the wider the range of its interpretation; the wider the range of its interpretation, the greater the responsibility of the director to the author. The director of *The Second Mrs. Tanqueray* cannot stray very far in his interpretation, his vision is bounded by the range of the play rather than by the abundance of stage directions; but the director of *Hamlet* can stray very far indeed, and can easily lose touch with his author, as his imagination flies out into the vaster vision that the author has opened up for him.

There are no rules, except the rules of conscience and common sense, which limit the extent of the director's vision. Those critics who are anxious to have things neatly labelled, so that they can have a safe anchor to which to tie their criticisms, will tend to decry any new interpretation by the director, but I hope I have shown you that this interpretation is necessary to the author and the test of any interpretation is its impact on the audience. If what we have seen when we go to see a performance of *Hamlet* has illuminated the play for us, revealed a truth which time has blurred, moved us more than before, if all this has happened to us without our being disturbed by extraneous inventions by the director, or interference with the text, then the vision is working in the right direction.

To sum up, we can say that there are no rules we can easily formulate to guide the relation between director and author, and that a special responsibility devolves upon the former in respect of the latter. For the author, be he alive or dead, to hand his play to a director is an act of faith; in return he expects the director to interpret his play to the audience, whether it be in Siam or Iceland, with loyalty to his intentions, and at the same time in a form which is theatrically acceptable to that audience.

But in his desire to serve the author as well as the audience, the director must not attempt to impose upon the play a significance which it does not possess, nor to give it an ethical, political, social or any other purpose, to enhance its importance or popularity. Stanislavsky in his production of Tchechov was able to point a social moral from this author's plays which well suited the Zeitgeist of pre-revolutionary Russia. He believed this social satire to be inherent in the plays, though Tchechov himself was probably less aware of it than his director. Tchechov wrote of the people who surrounded him—a society on the verge of a profound social upheaval. He neither advocated the revolution that was to come, nor did he condemn the old order that was passing. He loved both Trofimov with his dreams and Gaev with his billiards, but when he puts into Trofimov's mouth these words—'Here is happiness—here it comes! If we never see it—if we may never know it—what does it matter? Others will see it after us'—he was, though perhaps unconsciously, portraying a hope, a belief, felt by so many young idealists of pre-revolutionary Russia. Inevitably such words would send a thrill through the soul of the audience who went to the Moscow Arts Theatre in the early years of the Revolution; inevitably the actor who spoke them and the dicrector who trained his actors responded to this appeal and gave them a special significance—a significance which at the time was truly theatrical, but which to-day no longer is so. But Stanislavsky was right in his day to underline the significance of this speech.

The first Shakespeare play to be presented in Berlin after the war was *Macbeth*; in the last scene the director of the play made a specially dramatic moment of Macduff's last speech:

> 'Hail, King! for so thou art; behold where stands
> The usurper's cursed head; the time is free.'

for this panegyric of the victory of freedom over tyranny and over an age of murder and fear was true, not only to the intention of the play itself, but to the contemporary feeling of the audience—or so we hope. True, that is, within the meaning of theatrical truth.

Such examples which lie within the purpose, either conscious or subconscious, of the text are rightful interpretations, but there are lamentable examples of unwarranted impositions by the director with the purpose of exciting the popular taste of the day. Such impositions may suit the Zeitgeist of the audience, but they are false to the Zeitgeist of the author.

You may ask why, if it is wrong to impose an extraneous interpretation on a play, is it not also wrong to impose on it artistic or theatrical embellishments which were not envisaged by the author? What does loyalty to the author really mean? Are we to confine our productions of such plays as *The Comedy of Errors*, *Two Gentlemen of Verona*, or *Love's Labour's Lost* to the bare text, or are we permitted to embellish them so that they are a pleasure instead of a penance to the audience? Some critics may reply that these are apprentice plays, and nobody

44

will be offended if the director exercises a little licence. Yet, if it is true that they are not very good plays, why perform them at all? What right has the director to decorate them with music and songs in order to make them acceptable?

Instead of answering this question, I will draw your attention to a more mature play by Shakespeare on which, it might be said, there is no reason for the director to impose an extraneous imagination, and yet it is a play which, of all Shakespeare's plays, has been the most embellished. I refer to *A Midsummer Night's Dream*.

In the early 19th century, under the influence of the romantic movement, *A Midsummer Night's Dream* began to assume a popularity which it had not enjoyed since the Elizabethan era, and possibly had never enjoyed before. This renaissance of the play began in Germany, influenced by the new music which Mendelssohn had written for it. Mendelssohn's music, together with the opportunities that the play gave for ballet, picturesque scenery, beautiful costumes, mechanical devices and atmospheric lighting, stamped it with an aura completely foreign to its Elizabethan atmosphere, but most acceptable to the Zeitgeist of 19th-century romanticism both in Germany and in England. With the technical developments of the stage: with revolving stages, flying devices, waterfalls and electric lights, the play became less of *A Midsummer Night's Dream* than of a director's dream. The audience of to-day, habituated to this lush entertainment with its coy Puck, often played by an attractive young lady, its fairy ladies in diaphanous skirts and transparent wings, will resent any attempt to rescue the play from the impositions of this miscalled traditional treatment. Yet the play was not intended to be a sort of Christmas pantomime, complete with transformation scenes, nor a German operetta.

A Midsummer Night's Dream is an allegory of romantic love as viewed by a Renaissance playwright. It is a subject which occupies a predominant place in Elizabethan poetry. It is filled

with the alternation of torment and happiness which character-
ises those sonnets the author addressed to the dark lady. This
Renaissance philosophy of love lays down that love-making
is a madness from which man and woman cannot escape and
that this struggle between male and female, this deliberate
wounding of the heart, is a necessary process which can only
be ended by the estate of marriage. The subject of the play is
the jealousy, misunderstanding and reconciliation that accom-
panies the process of mating. As in *Love's Labour's Lost*,
Shakespeare sees the mating of male and female as a period of
madness—a feverish intoxication which cannot be cured by
reason, for the power of reason cannot operate if man falls a
victim to love.

> 'Lovers and madmen have such seething brains,
> Such shaping fantasies, that apprehend
> More than cool reason ever comprehends.'

The season of wooing is a nightmare in which the normal code
of human behaviour is reversed, or it is a furious dance in
which the partners, Demetrius and Helena, Lysander and
Hermia, sway from deepest loathing to intense idolatory, as
their temperatures sore up and down from hot to cold.
Eventually, with the coming of dawn, the Midsummer nightmare ends, the mating is concluded, the females accept their
males and sweet reason returns with the discipline of matri-
mony. Theseus and Hippolyta represent this state of maturity
to which man and woman must eventually come after their
temporary nightmarish journey in the wood of these primeval
passions. The powers of nature, to which men and women
temporarily abandon themselves, are of course the fairy people
ruled by Oberon and Titania. The eternal alternation of harmony and discord in nature is represented by the quarrels of
these elemental spirits who can influence man to his ill, once he
allows himself to stray into the kingdom where unbridled
passion holds sway. Even the sensible, earthy craftsmen can fall
victims to the whims and witchcraft of these mischievous

spirits of earth and air. To Shakespeare and his contemporaries, more especially to the people of the country, the presence of such spirits was strongly felt. These descendants of an older religion had remained hidden in the bracken and bushes of the countryside, changing their names and shapes as they eluded the power of the Church and the debunking of science. So Oberon and his team avoid the light of day:

'And we fairies, that do run
By the triple Hecate's team
From the presence of the sun,
Following darkness like a dream . . .'

These primeval forces of nature are for Shakespeare a danger to be overcome, for they are the symbol of the madness which besets the lunatic, the lover and the poet, taking away the cool reason which is man's God-like attribute and submitting him to the passions, the frenzies and the excessive imagination which distort his views on life; making him imagine a bush to be a bear, or blinding his vision so that he sees Helen's beauty in a brow of Egypt. There is in this play a distant association with the Greek Baccinalia and the fertility cult, and a close association with the May-time and Harvest ceremonies of our own countryside. The play was probably commissioned as part of the revels that accompanied a marriage celebration in some great Elizabethan household:

'To the best bride-bed will we
Which by us shall blessed be:
And the issue there create
Ever shall be fortunate.'

These concluding lines of Oberon have the significance of the fertility rites which are still found in the less sophisticated communities of Europe.

It is to travel very far indeed to associate such rites with the pretty young ladies who tripped about our Victorian stage, or suspended themselves in mid-air on the wires of Mr. Kirby's flying ballet. I doubt if this allegory of mating is really suitable to receive a 'U' certificate and to be performed by the junior classes of our schools.

Yet, here we must pause for we are on the horns of a dilemma. The Victorian treatment of *The Dream* with Mendelssohn's romantic music, with its dances and processions, is at its best very beautiful and, as directed by Reinhardt (and by Guthrie in his first production of this play), it can classify as a work of theatrical art. But is this treatment a true interpretation of the author's play? And if not, can we have a work of theatrical art which is at the same time a distortion of the author's intention? The answer is, of course, yes; just as we can have a fine portrait which bears no resemblance to the sitter; truth in art is a relative term. But the director cannot lay claim to the same freedom as the painter, for his job is to interpret creatively, not merely to create. Should he, therefore, embellish or distort the author's play in order to make it a work of art? But, if he is allowed by some critics to embellish a poor play, why should he not embellish a good play? Those critics may say that a good play needs no attention from the director, but isn't *A Midsummer Night's Dream* a good play? And do not the same critics endorse its embellishment and even hint that *The Dream* without pretty decoration is almost sacrilege? All I can do to answer these questions is to sit like the judge and sum up the situation to you, the jury, asking you to give the verdict.

Now, I want you to listen very carefully to what I have to say, for you will shortly be asked to pronounce a judgement of guilty or innocent upon the prisoner at the bar. The prisoner is accused of unethical conduct in that, having advertised the production of a play by one—William Shakespeare—entitled *A Midsummer Night's Dream*, he has conspired to defraud the author of his intention by substituting an artistic creation of his own. The accused is, as we know, responsible both to his author and to his audience, for his task is to interpret the work of the former to the latter. This he does through his vision of the

48

play; and this vision must take into account both the Zeitgeist of the author and that of the audience. This act of vision is allowed to take the form of a personal interpretation of the author's play, and as such it will vary widely according to the imaginative powers and temperament of the director. But the stage, unlike painting, is an interpretative art, and the accused cannot lay claim to the same imaginative freedom as a Rembrandt or a Rubens, for the latter are creative artists, and the accused is not, at least not wholly so.

Now Shakespeare wrote this play as an allegory of romantic love, and it is steeped in the philosophy and temper of the Elizabethan outlook. The accused has interpreted it as a fairy fantasy and steeped it in the fancies of Victorian romanticism—a romanticism which was in essence and feeling totally different from that of the author. The defence is said to have made out of it a work of theatrical art, and I do not wish to fog the issue by saying that he might also have made out of it a work of theatrical art if he had interpreted it in a form closer to its original purpose, for we have no evidence of this; and we must admit that we no longer hold close communion with the unseen powers of nature in quite the same way as Shakespeare's contemporaries did, nor have we the same outlook on love as the Elizabethan poets. The defence claims that the accused satisfied the Zeitgeist of the 19th-century audience and, apparently, still does so to-day. The prosecution, whilst admitting that the play still pleases a Victorian-conscious audience, denies that it is a truthful interpretation of the author.

You must bear in mind that if you find this man guilty of the unethical conduct of which he is accused, you may well be condemning in him the whole theory of Gordon Craig, and of other great men, whose work is founded on the belief that the Art of the Theatre is an art in its own right, and who have exemplified this in our modern theatre. But you must also bear in mind that, in placing a play in the hands of a director, the author—be he living or dead—is performing an act of trust, which places a grave responsibility upon the shoulders of the director. I feel sure you will equally bear in mind the need for theatrical truth in all things connected with the stage and will not allow irrelevant academic truth to prejudice you against the accused who stands by this defence of theatrical truth. I must remind you of the whole ethics of the stage, and of what we mean by this act of interpretation of the author's work. If I do so in somewhat fanciful language, you will not be misled, for you have already listened patiently to the arguments that have been advanced to-day on this vexed question of interpretation.

'In the beginning was the word', and what follows is the interpretation of the word. Widely different in many continents; under the palm trees of Bali or the oak trees of England, in the snows of the North or the pagodas of the East; widely different down the ages from the spacious arenas of Greece, through the dark passages of the Middle Ages to the neon lights of Shaftesbury Avenue; in space and in time the interpretation of the word has altered, and must alter, if the word is to live. Who is, then, to set up a boundary to this interpretation? What critic anxious to find formulas has the right to say, this you shall do and this you shall not. False prophets have arisen who have distorted the word and turned it to evil; false prelates have tried to arrest its interpretation so that the life fell from it and the people believed it was dead. But if truth is in the word —truth not for one day but for all ages—then the only boundaries to its interpretation are the loyalty and love of those who interpret it. Are you prepared to admit such an interpretation does, in fact, constitute lack of loyalty or love for the author?

. . . .

It appears you were unable to reach a unanimous verdict; I am not surprised. You will now see that in dealing with the subject of interpretation we are dealing with a subject which has few rules, and about which it is almost impossible to theorise. Once again I must emphasise that what we see when we go to the theatre, and what we do when we act in it, is of infinitely greater value than anything we can say about it. If we had seen this performance of *A Midsummer Night's Dream*, with its ballet, its transformation scenes, and its music by Mendelssohn, instead of discussing it in the abstract, we might have been able to reach a unanimous verdict as to whether the director had interpreted the play satisfactorily in terms of a modern audience, or whether he had deliberately misrepresented the author by imposing upon the text a spurious romantic interpretation which belied its intrinsic philosophy.

You may say that the average member of the audience has not studied the author's text, and, if it is a new play, he has no chance of knowing what the author intended. It is, therefore, sometimes unjust to the author for the play to be judged solely by the interpretation of the director and the actors. Maybe it is, maybe there are some new plays and some revivals which fail because of the interpretation, but there are others which succeed because of it. All we can say at the moment is that the director is on his honour to interpret the author's text as he sees it. If, for him, *A Midsummer Night's Dream* appears as a fairy fantasy, a pantomime, a masque, an allegory of romantic love, or a romantic operetta; if he believes that its interpretation to a contemporary public is best served by a performance in the open air or in a conventional theatre or on an open stage or on the films, on television or on sound recording, he is at liberty to so interpret it, providing he is working from an inner conviction as an artist, and not merely as a showman intent on drawing the crowds.

We are not in a position to say how *A Midsummer Night's Dream* ought to be produced. It may very well be that our so-called Elizabethan production is as far from the truth as the Victorian romantic conception. If I am asked to give an answer, however, I would say that neither way is the best way to-day. The director should, I believe, endeavour to interpret a play in terms of the present, and neither Elizabethan nor Victorian productions are in the spirit of the times in which we live. My plea, then, is that the director's task is not to imitate the past, but to use his imagination to interpret the author in terms of the modern Art of the Theatre.

If the author objects to the imaginative interpretation of his play, then why is he writing for a medium which requires it? Would he not do better to write novels or essays or poetry, where he is in direct contact with the audience? Once again, I must emphasise that the author is only a collaborator in the Art of the Theatre; his work is not that art itself; no more is that of the director, the designer or the composer, but what about the actor?

The Director and the Actor

'THE Art of the Theatre', said Granville Barker, 'is the art of acting first, last and all the time.' This statement might be misleading, because it could be used as a cover for advocating the virtuoso acting of the romantic school which starred the solo performance of one actor and deliberately suppressed the contribution of the team; or because it could be argued as a reason for altering the play's text to suit the actor's performance. Barker's statement is a condensation of the meaning of the Art of the Theatre—an attempt to define this art in a sentence that is easily understood. Such attempts at clarification are more often than not misleading.

What this statement means, at least what it means to me is that the Art of the Theatre must be judged by what happens on the stage in front of the audience—rather than what the author or the director or the stage designer may have intended to happen. It is the practice of the theatre, rather than the theory, that is its art, and the practice is performed not by the author, nor by the director, but by the actors. The director has, in fact, little power to control what happens when the actors meet the audience, his job is to prepare the way for this meeting and this he does by interpreting the text which the author has provided, assessing, as far as he is able, the reaction of the audience to it, and helping the actor to adjust his performance accordingly. But all the meticulous planning of manager,

53

author, director, designer, costumier, property man and stage manager can be brought to nought, if the meeting between the actor and his audience fails to give birth to a living performance. So what Barker's statement means is, that the practice of the theatre is determined more by the actors than by the author, the director, or the other contributors. But how far does the director control the actors?

The main control over the actors is exercised through the casting of the play. I sometimes wonder if in fact correct casting of a play is not the main contribution a director can make to the success of its performance. I do not mean type casting, as it is practised sometimes in the West End theatre and more frequently in films, in which old So-and-so is always cast as a butler and Miss Doings as a glamorous minx. Type casting of artists is not only bad for the artist, preventing him or her from developing the art of acting, but bad for the play, because it tends to impose a ready-made character on it, instead of allowing the characterisation to rise out of the text. Actors who rely on their personality, rather than on their art, are incapable of playing a character written by the author, they can only play the specialised character they themselves have invented. Their excuse is that the public likes to see them as themselves; this is not acting, any more than is the appearance of the bearded-woman at a side-show at Blackpool.

Casting a play correctly is an art in itself, and to be an expert in it the director needs to have more than a conventional knowledge of an actor's personality, as well as the power to draw out the hidden talent that he knows the actor possesses. This question of hidden talent in an actor, whether it be through the discovery of new players of talent, or whether it be through the display of an unknown talent in a familiar player, is one of the theatre's most potent secret weapons. There is nothing so likely to please an audience than the feeling it is participating in an event. A new face or a new mask on an old face is sound showmanship. I quote as examples Claire Bloom as Juliet,

54

Audrey Hepburn as Ondine, Dorothy Tutin in *The Living Room*; or as George Robey as Falstaff and Donald Wolfit as Lord Ogilvie in *The Clandestine Marriage*. On the other hand, if the experiment fails to come off, it can be one of the theatre's most tragic experiences. It seems strange, perhaps, that we should advocate novelty rather than proved worth in acting, but novelty is an essential part of the theatre which still retains much of the appeal of the fair ground booth where novelty reigns supreme. The stage must always renew itself, if it is to live, and repetition, whether it be of a style of production or of an over-familiar performance by an actor, is no contribution to this vital and illuminating art.

But in Britain the director seldom has complete freedom to cast to the best possible advantage. The conditions of the long-run London theatre, as well as of the touring theatre, demand the presence of one or more star players to serve the requirements of the box office, and star casting may sometimes be unsuitable for the best interpretation of a part. On the other hand, if the play is performed in repertory, the director is severely limited in his casting by the need to use the contracted players of the company. Miscasting is more frequent in repertory than in the long-run theatre; for we can fortunately say that in the theatre, as apart from films, stars are not made by publicity agents, but by their merits as players, and a star artist of the theatre is unlikely to risk his or her reputation by playing a part which is clearly unsuitable. On the other hand if repertory casting is not always ideal, it has the advantage of teamwork and is blessed by the feeling of security, which allows actors and actresses to develop their parts without worrying unduly about the success or failure of one particular performance. But whether the director has all the freedom he desires or not, he does largely control the actors through the way in which the play is cast.

Let us now follow the director through the main stages of his work with the actor and see how far he can, or should, shape the course of events. We must, of course, imagine that the director has reasonable time to rehearse the play; and, what is equally important, reasonable time to prepare it before rehearsals begin. Neither serious production, nor serious acting, is possible in conditions of weekly repertory. All the director can do in so short a time is to perform the function of a stage-manager, ensuring that the stage directions of the acting edition are adhered to, and the furniture correctly placed. All the actor can do is to learn his lines and turn on his well-known impersonation of a man about town or an old colonel or a country curate, or whatever is relatively closest to the author's character. Let us imagine, however, that our rehearsals are to be conducted in civilised circumstances and that both actors and director are to have a chance of doing a serious job of work. The director must first come to terms with his text, before he calls his rehearsals—that is, he must establish his vision of the play.

Having once decided the style and form of his production and, if the author is living, and this is to be the first performance of the play, having secured his agreement for the way he is going to treat it, the director approaches the designer and explains his ideas. Together they work out ground plans of the scenery. If the play has many scenes in it, as in the Elizabethan plays, the director and designer will endeavour to solve the problem of continuity; avoiding, if they can, breaking the flow of the action by unnecessary scene changes. How much or how little the director suggests to the designer must depend on the qualities and abilities of each of them. Ideally the director and the designer are the same person, as in the case of Gordon Craig; where this cannot be so, then they must endeavour to work as one mind, each contributing to a single vision. Probably the director will suggest the broad lines of the style to be followed, leaving the details to the designer. In designing the scenery, the director will, however, concentrate on the actor's interests, ensuring that the ground plan gives ample scope for movement and intimacy in the right places; that windows, doors and furniture are placed where they are most wanted, and where they will also fit the choreography of the play, which is now beginning to take shape in his mind. He will also keep a careful eye on the costume designs and, if he is wise, take the principal actors into his confidence over these from the beginning, for the actor must have a physical as well as a mental approach to his part. Some actors require to settle the question of physical appearance before they can find the necessary stimulus to search for the character they are studying; and, difficult as it may seem to the designer, he must take the actor's views into account and not try to impose a character upon him which is foreign to his personality. Bottom's first question when he eventually accepts to play the part of Pyramus is, 'What beard were I best to play it in?' To which Quince wisely replies, 'Why, what you will', leaving Bottom to work this question out for himself. In fact, like all matters in the theatre, costume and make-up is a matter of talking it out, arriving at a just decision after taking all views into account and keeping an open mind for as long as possible.

Having settled these details to his and the designer's satisfaction, he now starts to plot the movement of his players. This is a laborious task, for the director must constantly have in mind the interests of author, audience and to some extent, designer. He will first of all have in mind the style of his choreography; if the play is to be treated with realism, then the movement must appear to be natural; if it is to be stylised, then the degree of its stylisation must be settled. Acting is, after all, only a convention, a form of contract between actor and spectator. It is never complete naturalism, or we should neither hear nor see properly what the actor was saying or doing. In his vision of the play the director has already settled just what the style is to be, and so long as he adheres rigidly to it, the audience will accept the contract that has been made. For example, in a Chinese play the audience accept the fact that the players have

continuity from Key on the to key work [handwritten margin note]

This must be the important thread. [handwritten note]

neither properties nor scenery and a gallop once round the stage will represent a journey or horseback; the convention has been settled from the beginning and the audience accept their half of the contract. But if the play is realistically written and we provide the actors with realistic surroundings, the audience will not accept it if the actors spread out their arms and say they are flying to America. In working out the actors' movement, the director must make sure that he is not asking the actor to do anything which will shatter this contract which must at all costs be kept with the spectator.

Next he will be careful to plot the actors' positions so that they are always in correct relationship to each other; for instance, an intimate conversation between two players must not take place over the heads of two or three other persons. He must make sure that his actors do not move too much, so that the author's words are lost, or too little, so that they send the audience to sleep, for the art of maintaining the audience's concentration is neither to move too much nor too little. Actors must never appear to be moving around to get out of each other's way, though that may be precisely what they are doing. Every move must have an apparent reason, either practical—to fetch an umbrella, to draw the curtains, to go out, or to sit down—or significant to attract the audience's attention to a key phrase or action. High-lighting of important moments in the play must be carefully and sparingly reflected in the positions of the actors; carefully so that the same dominating position is not used for every important moment; sparingly so that only the key situations are high-lighted, otherwise the value of such dominance is lost. The leading actor or actress is popularly supposed to demand his or her right of standing or sitting in the middle of the stage, slightly upstage of everyone else, and staying there no matter who is leading the dialogue. Such behaviour does, of course, happen, but only among the dying race of unintelligent players; it is the director's authority which tactfully persuades such actors to take their places as members of the team. But the upstage centre position is not necessarily the dominant one; soliloquies and low comedy —particularly the comedy of Shakespeare's clowns—should be acted downstage, near the footlights if it is a picture-frame theatre; the music-hall comedian knows the value of this position.

Grouping of characters, giving momentary pictures which set the style or atmosphere at a particular moment, is important, but the director should constantly be aware of the need to compose a picture with his actors—the actors forming a pattern on the stage in harmony with each other and in proportion with the scenery, for harmony and proportion are an aid to concentration. Such compositions must always be naturally formed, without forcing the movement or making the audience aware that the director is deliberately imposing a pattern. Crowds must also be dealt with, but I advise the director to do most of his crowd work on the stage after he has accommodated the leading actors, for crowd work should be influenced by the key actors, and not influence them; Mark Antony must be dealt with before we deal with his auditors, lest the latter impose a pattern on the performance of the former. There are some directors who excel at manœuvring a crowd on the stage, and, indeed, fascinating and exciting evolutions can be performed by a large crowd, but the danger of exaggerating the importance of such effects is considerable, and a director must remember that he is not on the stage to show off his skill to the audience. His function is to serve the author, the actors and the audience, and never to use the stage as a canvas for his own embroidery. A good production is one that passes unobserved; a good director is one who does not sign his productions.

Now to plan all this movement before the director is in actual contact with the actors in rehearsal may seem to be a little complicated. Shaw explains how it can be done with a set of chessmen to represent the players and a few child's bricks to indicate the scenery or the furniture. Personally I find chessmen a little confusing, as I never remember which pawn is meant to be which actor. But as a child I used to collect wooden Swiss bears, to each one I gave a distinct character of its own, and these I now keep in constant employment. I sometimes wonder what leading artists would think if they saw themselves in such disguise, perched on toy sofas in my preliminary efforts to work out their positions. As the director with the aid of chessmen, or bears, or simply with a pencil and paper, sketches out his stage movement, he carefully plots all this in his prompt copy which becomes the score of the production. An example of such a score, worked out with meticulous care, is to be found in the published edition of Stanislavsky's production of *The Seagull*, a work which took the director four weeks to complete and which the company were able to put into practice before Stanislavsky appeared to conduct rehearsals, so carefully was it annotated. Besides stage movement, the director's score should contain the cues for particular stage effects, such as 'a tolling bell' or 'a distant violin', which we call noises off. These the director will later discuss and farm out to the stage-manager; also music and lighting cues, each to be discussed with the relative experts and farmed out to them. A good score will also include indications of tempo, such as pauses, passages to be taken quickly and passages which must be given special significance. This score, or prompt book, is usually filed away after the production is over in some corner of the theatre where it gradually accumulates dust; and is eventually thrown away with the receipts of yester-year. If the play is published in an acting edition—a deplorable practice—it may earn the director five guineas for its use by the publishers. I maintain that all prompt books, unless they are to be kept as exhibits in a theatre museum, should be promptly destroyed. A director's prompt book relates only to his personal direction of a particular play, with a particular cast, in a particular setting and at a particular point of time. It can, or should have, no relation to another director's work on the same play with another cast, in another setting, at another point of time. Every approach to a play must be an individual approach and imitation or reproduction, has no place in an art as ephemeral as that of the theatre. In any case, if reproduction is really considered a legitimate form of direction, five guineas is hardly a fair fee to pay a director for the copyright of his work.

Next to control of the actors through the casting, I consider the most valuable contribution the director can make to a production lies in the clarity with which he tells the story. The ability to do this is a little difficult to define. Melodramas, for instance, depend for their entertainment value almost exclusively upon the skill with which the narrative is developed. In the detective play, in which the surprise ending or the unmasking of the villain is so obviously important that it may sometimes have to take precedence over truthful characterisation, the skill of the actors and the director will be measured by the way they can sustain the tension and prevent the audience from solving the mystery before the climax arrives. In other plays, however, the characterisation may seem more important than the narrative—for instance in Tchechov, where the actors and director can so easily slur over the slender threads of the story in their enthusiasm over atmosphere and characterisation. Unless in *The Cherry Orchard* the director insists on underlining those passages which deal with the impending auction of the property and stresses the social aspect and the decadence of the pre-revolutionary landowner class, which amounts almost to a mental illness in their inability to face reality, the play becomes a feckless and meandering affair, in which the audience can see no point of contact with their own experience, promptly labelling it as one of those gloomy Russian plays.

In the poetic plays of Shakespeare the literary qualities can too easily take prominence over the plot; the theory being that everyone knows the story anyway. *Hamlet* seems doomed to be treated as a play of personality, or a display of personality, and the story, which is fundamentally a story of revenge, is lost. The director is so anxious to show off his leading actor in his purple passages that the relation of those passages to the action is often forgotten. A play like *The Merchant of Venice* is sometimes considered by the sophisticated to be such a poor piece of dramatic narrative, except in its trial scene, that the less we follow the story of Portia and the caskets the better. Too often the director either presents the casket scenes in such a way that Bassanio knows all the time the secret of the lead casket, which makes him into a hypocrite, or Portia into a cheat, or he will introduce so much spectacle into the arrival of these suitors that no one worries very much about the naive little plot. But, although the audience may be temporarily blinded by the splendid costumes, the processions, music and ornate movement, it will leave only partially satisfied with the play if it cannot follow the story.

A play is basically a narrative; its origin, either in this country or abroad, was for the purpose of instruction, its task was to tell a story in the most palatable and impressive way. To some extent the religious picture could do this, but its scope was limited by its static nature; the play was introduced as the most potent and graphic form of story-telling to an illiterate audience. So in the earliest days the story was more potent than the characters which were stock figures taken from the Bible or popular legend. The actor's main purpose was to illustrate the action, rather than to explain its motivation, through the characters. In the early mystery play, the actor playing the part of Abraham must show how he nearly came to slay Isaac, he is not asked to delve into the psychological reasons for doing so, and Stanislavsky's method will be little use in such a case. What the actors of such a play must possess, beyond their own histrionic powers, is a belief in the effectiveness of the story, and an understanding of how to tell it dramatically, for only if the actors believe in a play can that play be communicated to the audience. However much the play form may have developed, taking on literary or social or psychological embellishments, it remains basically a form of story-telling and this story-telling in the theatre must be a primary concern of the actors. Now in a film this is not so; it is perfectly possible for a film to grip and hold the attention of an audience without the actors knowing the story of the film, or indeed being more than superficially interested in it. To use a theatrical expression we can sum it up by saying it is not the actors who 'put across' a film, but the director and his technicians. On the stage, the director and the technicians can only provide the framework, it is the actors who put the story across, and to this extent Granville Barker is right in saying that the Art of the Theatre is the art of acting. But it is the director's job to see that the actors do put the story across; that they do not forget the basis of theatrical art in their desire to display the art of acting. I would therefore advise the director to underline those passages in his score which are key points in telling the play's story.

I must make it clear that not all directors do, in fact, prepare a score. Some prefer to rely on the inspiration of the moment; allowing the play to form its own choreography in rehearsal. The success of this method, which has the value of greater spontaneity, must depend on the ability of the director to form quick judgements and to stick by them, for nothing is more tiresome, nor a greater waste of time, than to have a constant experiment being performed while the director makes up his mind which movement is best. Actors, I believe, like a combination of both methods: set choreography for the first days of rehearsal to allow them to explore the framework of the production and the boundaries of their part in it, and reasonable liberty to alter and extemporise their movement as they begin to find the shape of the production. But whether the director prepares a score, or whether he relies on the spontaneous method, he must come to rehearsal with a general vision, either in his head or on paper, and he must make sure that every member of the cast understands what that vision is and what his own part in it is to be.

The director must remember that the first rehearsal of the play is a considerable ordeal to the actor. The actor comes to his first rehearsal, more often than not, with no very clear idea how he is going to play his part; or, if he has an idea, he will probably find the inspiration which seemed so definite in the privacy of his rooms completely eludes him when he is faced with his fellows. The larger the part, the more acute will be his agony; for whereas the small part players seem confident and efficient, the key players will appear clumsy and awkward, totally incapable of holding the tension, pointing the comedy or raising the emotion. But the director will know that a polished reading of a part rarely means an inspired performance of it. The polished reader has usually done all the work he is capable of doing on the characterisation before the rehearsals start. He has no further contribution to make, neither in light of the director's score, nor in relation to the other performances. He has provided the external gloss before he has had time to digest the internal truth and the first reading of his part which has been given with such effect is his final performance of it.

The director, then, must try to avoid giving his players the impression that they are on trial during the early rehearsals. He must do nothing to force them into a hasty and ill-digested characterisation. His task will be to lead them slowly into the play, giving them time to look round and take in their surroundings, encouraging them to question the reason for this or that position or movement, so that they fully absorb his score before they begin to create their own contribution to it. My own method is to prepare a preface to introduce the play to the players. This I read to them at their first rehearsal coupled with a general description of how the production is to be staged. At this first rehearsal I like to have all the principal participants present, besides the actors. Ideally the author should be there as well as the designer, the composer, the principal costumier, the stage-manager, and the property master. It will probably be the only time the full team will meet together before the dress rehearsals and it is important that not only does everyone concerned in the production learn exactly what effect is being aimed at, so that he or she can see how the work they have to do must fit into a harmonious picture, but that the actor has an opportunity to discuss such ideas as he may have about his costume or properties with the experts who are to make them before it is too late to make changes.

My preface covers such notes on the play as may be of general use to the actor, though it does not set out to be too directorial; for the actor should be encouraged to seek out his sources for himself, if sources are available. This preface covers my own personal vision of the play and indicates the mood or atmosphere, the purpose or style, that I propose to develop in my production of it. In it I try to indicate the broad lines of characterisation that I want the actors to follow, pointing out the textual references to support my views. Again I would emphasise that this is not intended as a literary analysis, nor as a hard and fast formula from which the actor cannot escape. Though in the case of certain characters which are not easily explainable, or of which two or more interpretations can be given, I definitely indicate the characterisation I want followed in my preface. For instance, the character of Fabian in *Twelfth Night*, or Don Armado and Moth in *Love's Labour's Lost*, are open to a variety of interpretations. No doubt this was not so in Shakespeare's day, but to-day the key to these characters is lost, and a new one must be found, if they are to be made living to a contemporary audience. This preface will probably be followed by a reading of the play, either by the author, the director or the players. Some directors require their actors to read the play for several sessions, before allowing them to plot their moves. The Moscow Arts Theatre, for instance, spend weeks reading and discussing the significance, atmosphere and characterisation. Much must depend on the time factor of rehearsals, but in general it will be found that the more the play is discussed and understood in the early period of rehearsal, the less waste of time will occur during the period of plotting the movement. If the actors thoroughly understand and digest the play and the reasons for the interpretation that is being given it, they will avoid those misunderstandings which can give rise to controversy at a later stage.

The following rehearsals will be taken up with plotting the movement, a task which takes several days; and, whilst this is in progress, the players will be discovering for themselves the limits of their performances and evolving the main lines of their approach to their parts. All this we might call the first stage of rehearsal, a period during which the director will be the dominant force, providing the actor with the framework inside which he is to work. During this stage the director will not be, as is popularly supposed, sitting at the back of the theatre, shouting instructions down a megaphone. His place is on the stage with the players, moving amongst them, indicating movement and sometimes performing it, never far enough away from his players to be insensitive of their reactions or their difficulties.

Often enthusiastic playgoers have begged me for permission to visit a rehearsal, little realising that they will in fact glean nothing from this, beyond seeing what appears to be a gaggle of Trades Union delegates discussing a controversial resolution in the lunch-hour break—except, of course, that actors are not so well dressed. For the director does not adopt the methods of a school-master lecturing a class; his instructions are given privately to one or two actors; nor will the actors be giving moving performances of their parts. This is the initial period, a period during which the actor is absorbing the material out of which he is going to carve his performance. Yet it should not be imagined that, whilst working within this

framework, the actor should be subjected to an iron dictatorship. It is, of course, possible for a director to set up as a
dictator and impose a performance upon his actors, rather than
eliciting a performance from them. Such methods are rarely
successful.

There is a story told about Ellen Terry, who once found
herself being directed by a notoriously authoritative director
who gave her minute directions for every move, gesture and
inflexion she was to make. 'Yes, Mr. Blank, I think I understand,' she replied. 'I am to move here and touch this and look
there. And then,' she added sweetly, 'I must do that little
bit extra, mustn't I? For which you are going to pay me
much more than any of the others.' It is precisely that 'little
bit extra' which finally counts. It is what the artist is, as well
as what he does, which counts on the stage. All the direction
in the world will not make a poor actor into a good one,
though it may make him into a tolerable one. Only the 'little
bit extra' will raise the actor into the top class, and only the
actor can provide it. The director is helpless to impose this
quality on an actor; it is often dangerous for him to try to
suggest ways and means by which the actor may be led to
find it. Once the actor has found this vital spark, which gives
life to his performance, he will, if he is a disciplined actor,
fit his performance into the framework. And the director,
if he is wise, will see to it that this vital spark is not smothered by any preconceptions of direction or any pet theories
which he—the director—considers more important than the
actor's skill. The director, then, must be very patient—that
patience which Shaw denies to the author—waiting for this
spark to be kindled. It may come before the play goes into
rehearsal, in which case the director must be prepared to give
it scope and room, altering his moves, if necessary, to fit the
actor's inspiration. It may not come at all, in which case the
director must see to it that his score is strongly enough built
to overcome the actor's lack of brilliance. If he is wise he will

keep in constant contact with his leading player or players, as he works on his score, explaining the main effects he hopes to make. In this way the player will study his part with his eye on the production into which he is going to fit in, and will not arrive at rehearsals with a mass of ideas which cannot be made to synchronise with those of the director. But it must be strictly understood by any director, no matter how eminent, that the relation between himself and the player is a two-way traffic. Once the director has made his blue print or explained his vision to the actor, he should be prepared to receive as much as he gives. The actor who is to play Hamlet or Macbeth or Oedipus or Tamburlaine will eventually have more to say about those characters than the director. It is the director's job to see, firstly, that the actor's contribution is in key with the score, and, secondly, that this contribution is shown to its best advantage. To this extent the director is both a trainer of, and an audience to, his actors. The greatest fault that can beset the director is lack of humility—a sort of pride which makes it difficult for him to accept advice and contributions from his players. When such a situation exists, it must be due to the director's lack of confidence in himself or in his material. A director cannot afford to lack confidence either in the play, his interpretation of it, his power to direct it and above all in the ability of his actors to act it. Naturally the director will have to exercise a more rigid control over some players than over others. The smaller characters cannot be allowed quite the same liberty of interpretation as he may give his key players, otherwise chaos will result, yet each must have some rein for creative interpretation.

The holding of the reins, allowing this player to plunge ahead and holding this one back, yet keeping the team within the limits of the road he has selected to travel; seeing that all contribute in equal measure to the task of pulling the play along it; is the main function of the director during the secondary stage of rehearsal. During this secondary stage the actor is gradually taking over the play from the director. It is the creative period of the play's birth. The first stage was largely technical, the director was setting up the skeleton of the play, drawing out the rough outlines in charcoal upon the canvas. Now come the actors with their high-lights and shades to paint in the picture, to cover the skeleton with flesh and to let the blood course through it. It is an exciting moment when life begins to flow through the play; there are days when nothing seems to happen; when the actors stumble through their words without bringing any new meaning to them; when the director requires both patience and confidence to restrain himself from forcing the issue and imposing performances on them. Then suddenly, perhaps late in the evening after an uneventful day, or early in the morning following a day of minor irritations and uninspired rehearsal, a sudden hush will descend on the dingy surroundings of the rehearsal room, something has happened, the actors have captured the mood, a scene is coming to life. It is an infectious moment, one actor will perhaps start it and like lightning the others will catch it—the key has been found. I remember when I was rehearsing a Russian play—*The Apple Orchards of Polovchansk*—how hopeless we found a certain scene to be. It seemed as if the characters were devoid of all reality, and no matter what emphasis we gave the lines or what moves we devised, the scene obstinately refused to come to life. Then suddenly during a rehearsal we heard the stage-manager playing over a record that was to be used in the production. It was a melancholy, haunting, Ukrainian folk-song, and we realised that this was the key to the scene. The actors started rehearsing to the background of the music; their tempo was slow and leisurely; there was no attempt to force the characterisation or the pace of the scene; the clouds lifted and the scene had a clear, haunting significance. There was no need to say anything, one could see the happiness on each actor's face, when we had finished. It was a simple answer, we had tried to force the tempo and we had lost the power to relax.

69

As the play begins to take its shape and the team begin to work together, knowing each other's paces, the director's grip on the reins must slacken, until he himself jumps from the driving-seat and watches the play speed along. His task is now to be an audience to his team, admiring their action, telling them when they are moving him, amusing him or gripping him, and when they are boring or confusing him. His position is now more withdrawn from his actors, he is no longer on the stage, but seated in the auditorium, getting a perspective view of the play. He is no longer constantly interrupting the actors, discussing points with them, or adjusting their positions. He has provided himself with a note-book perhaps, and is saving his criticism for the end of a scene or an act.

If a true spirit of co-operation has been engendered, the actor will now be eager to hear the director's reactions, and to listen to suggestions of how he can improve this effect or avoid that pitfall. The vision has now passed out of the director's hands and is being actively created by the players, whose knowledge of stage-craft and instinctive judgement of right and wrong will carry it through by themselves. Finally, the director will mount once more on to the driving-seat, as the play is put into dress rehearsals; for, during this final rough passage, the play may easily be shaken to pieces as it travels over the last hurdles of the road. It is now that all the various contributions are brought together in this, the third stage of rehearsal —the designer with his scenery and costumes, the stage-manager, the composer and the electrician, each with his special contribution. If the director is wise he will have been careful to introduce all these to the actors at different times during rehearsal, so that there are no undue shocks to disturb or destroy their performance. But, however careful he has been, some shocks are inevitable; the transition from rehearsal room to stage, if the play has been rehearsed outside the theatre in which it will eventually be played, can often prove disastrous. Rehearsal rooms, inadequately representing the acoustics of a theatre, are in fact one of the worst features of our theatre system, and the cause of much of the bad speaking of which critics so often complain. The West End play has often to be rehearsed in the upper room of a public house, which has no conceivable similarity with the conditions of a public theatre. However much the director may plead with his actors to broaden their effects, or to speak louder or more clearly, he will make little effect upon them, for to do so would be to kill the truth of their creation. Broad effects which rely on movement, action and rhetoric may not suffer from the artifice of playing them larger than their surroundings, but an intimate passage, be it the love scenes in *Romeo and Juliet* or a passage of Tchechov or a duet from Dodie Smith, cannot be rehearsed adequately in a room if they are projected for a stage. The actor's creative moments, once born in the rehearsal room, will take on the intimacy of these surroundings and will be in-effective and lacking in life when transferred to a larger arena. It may take many days before the performance born under such circumstances can adjust itself to its new surroundings.

The Old Vic, whose stage in a repertory season is constantly required by the stage-manager, suffers severely from this rehearsal room trouble. Although there is a reasonably large room in the building which can be used for rehearsals, the acoustics are atrocious. Every sound above a whisper is dis-torted into a full-throated roar. In consequence, however hard the actor tries to remember the requirements of the theatre, he is bound to pitch his voice in accordance with the acoustic properties of the room, if he is to rehearse with any degree of feeling or truth. By pitching his voice on a lower level, he develops certain characteristics of speech which are completely ineffective when transferred to the stage. If and when a National Theatre is built, it is to be hoped that the acoustic properties of the rehearsal rooms will be studied in relation to those of the auditorium; for nothing is more disheartening to a company than to find that all its hard work in rehearsal is nullified by the acoustics of the theatre in which it has to perform.

The meeting of actors with their scenery and costumes can also be disastrous, if the early rehearsals never take place in costume or on the set. Ideally at least two weeks of a four week rehearsal period should be spent in the theatre and rehearsed in the set with costumes resembling those to be worn in performance. The customary practice of a West End production is for the play to be rehearsed sometimes in a theatre (though rarely the one in which it is to be played), sometimes in a rehearsal room, and then to tour the provinces, in order to smooth off the rough edges and to test the public reaction. Necessary as such pre-West End tours may be, because of the inadequacy of our rehearsal system, they are by no means ideal.

It seems to me somewhat insulting to the provinces to use them merely as a rehearsal ground for inadequately prepared plays; moreover, the varying sizes of provincial theatres and the variety of audiences sometimes make the balance and tempo of the acting even more uncertain than the hazards of the rehearsal room; nor is the reaction of a provincial audience a certain guide to that of a highly specialised London first-night audience.

Once of the last tasks that the director will have to perform is to light the play. This is one of those technical subjects which a director must study, and it would require a lecture in itself to cover its principles. I would only wish now to draw your attention to those aspects of lighting which most concern the actor. There is nothing more exasperating for the actor than to come to the first lighting rehearsal and discover that all the positions he has so laboriously worked out on the director's instructions are plunged in murky darkness, and he is expected to alter them in order to conform to a fancy lighting plot which has now been worked out. Some adjustments of the actor in relation to the lights is almost inevitable; for lighting plots on paper never quite work out in practice, but the director must have his lighting plot in mind as he rehearses his play, and his positions should be adjusted accordingly. There is an almost inevitable tendency by both director and designer to underlight the actor in order to increase the atmosphere or effect of the scenery. On the other hand, the actor will, unless he is bathed in an arc lamp, nearly always complain that he can't find the lights. Many of these irritations can be avoided, if both director and designer have taken the lighting into account from the beginning, and have designed their setting so that it can be lit independently of the actors. The actor on the other hand should be told, in those scenes which require atmospheric lighting, exactly where the principal light sources will be, and the sort of intensity of light he can expect, so that he takes the lighting into account, as he works on the framework of the play.

Once the play has opened, the director has little more he can contribute. The actor has met the audience and is beginning to discover just how far he must shape his performance in order to gain his effects. The final stage of a play's birth is, in fact, achieved by this mysterious partnership between actor and audience, a partnership which occurs in no other dramatic medium yet invented. It is precisely this ephemeral but vital contact which gives life to a play, and which justified Granville Barker's remark that 'the art of the theatre is the art of acting first, last and all the time.'

The Director and the Public

A Survey of the Present and a Plan for the Future

WE finished our last discussion at the point where the actor made contact with the audience, a point at which the director's terms of reference are concluded.

We may wonder how it is that the director seems to know so little about the audience, that he is unable to assess accurately the reactions the play will receive in performance. How is it, for example, that he does not know in the early stages of rehearsal that the play will fail to please? The critics are constantly raising their eyebrows in amazement at the apparent inability of experienced managers and directors to realise that they are wasting their time and that of the cast in presenting a play, which any amateur would have rejected out of hand. Yet, if we knew the effect a play would have on the audience from the beginning, we might all be very rich people indeed. The truth is that, like gamblers, we cling to the sporting chance that a fine interpretation may overcome a play's textual weakness.

Once again, we must recognise that there are no certain rules of right and wrong in the theatre, no sure roads that lead to success or failure. There are some insurances we can take out; we can follow the practice of some London managements and load our plays with star artists. We can restrict our productions to the plays of established dramatists, such as Agatha Christie, Noel Coward or Terence Rattigan. But even these insurances cannot guarantee success, though they may minimise the risk. Yet the theatre cannot exist on such insurances alone, for there are not enough stars, nor enough established dramatists to go round. It must be prepared to take risks; to break the rules which are no rules; to try out new authors, actors, directors and designers; and, more important still, to try out new methods of attracting new audiences. It is this latter problem, more than any other, which seems to me of paramount importance to-day, for it receives the least attention. I consider it the most valuable contribution we can make to the theatre, and I propose to devote my last discussion to it.

Our public attitude towards the theatre is that it is, or should be, a self-supporting industry towards which the public has no obligations beyond the money it pays into the box-office. Yet this is not the attitude we adopt towards orchestras, museums, public libraries or art galleries. This attitude is not altogether surprising, since for centuries the theatre has been regarded as a disreputable profession into which no respectable parent would wish his child to enter. Yet, if the theatre is to be regarded as an industry, then it should adopt a realistic policy for its future development. This entails adequate training facilities, some measure of security for its employees, an experimental department, an audience research unit, a nation-wide publicity agency. Retrenchment by means of cutting expenditure or clinging to old formulas, which have proved popular in the past, is not a policy which, in the long run, can hope to succeed.

But before we discuss remedies, let us make a general survey of the state of our patient and see what deductions we can draw. At the top of the theatrical commonwealth in this country stands the commercial theatre of the West End of London, which, still, in our semi-nationalised state, is by far the most influential theatrical force. How long it is likely to remain so must depend on how far the public's purse can be stretched to meet the rising costs of production. The general tendency of production in the West End theatre is, as I said earlier, conservative. And this is principally due to the fact that the production of a play is an exceedingly costly business. Money has often to be found from outside backers, who, not unnaturally, interest themselves more in the particular investment they are making than in the general welfare of the theatre. As a result, experiment, either in the form of new leading actors, unusual play forms, or new production methods, is discouraged. But apart from the interests of the backer, neither the manager, the director nor the actor is anxious, in a world of financial values, to risk the blow to their reputation which a financial failure often implies. As a result, the London theatre has developed a formula of play presentation which is considered the safest way of minimising the risks.

This formula is seen in the solidly built realistic scenery which seems not to have developed at all since the end of the last century—indeed, stage realism can develop no further unless it grows a fourth wall and shuts the audience out altogether. Shakespearean production has, however, been rescued from the over-realistic tendencies which threatened to overwhelm it in the productions of Tree and the early 19th century. But the production of contemporary plays in this country and in America has evolved no new style to meet the changing times and the changing audience, as have the theatres of the Continent, more especially of Germany and Sweden and the avant-guard theatre of Paris. And although it would be wrong to condemn Anglo-American realism wholeheartedly, we must admit that never before was there so vast a gulf between the Art of the Theatre, as practised in these two countries, and the other contemporary arts of painting and sculpture. Even the Royal Academy is modernistic compared with most of the scenic art of our stages.

Although it would be wrong for the director or the scenic

artist to impose a non-realistic setting upon an essentially realistic play, yet there are instances when a more imaginative approach to realism would not be out of place. Eliot's plays seem to me to require more poetic staging than they receive in the West End, and it is noticeable how much more readily the public will respond to the general truth contained in them, once they are released from the particular identification that realism imposes. I have seen productions of Eliot, Ustinov and Fry on the Continent in which the plays have gained considerably from their release from the realistic, architectural setting of the West End.

Priestley's *An Inspector Calls* was presented in Moscow on a stage devoid of scenery, on which the actors were silhouetted against a lighted cyclorama. I am told by those who saw it that the play lost neither concentration, nor dramatic effect, but gained in the universal application of its theme. Too often the director adopts the conventional realistic formula, because he must play for safety. In this attitude he is supported by manager and star artist, who are anxious, at all costs, to avoid the stigma of 'experimental theatre'.

The insurance formula of the West End is also seen, as we have pointed out earlier, in the star system, which although it may add lustre to the event, acts as a brake on the growth of new talent. But we can take some comfort from the fact that the old formula of play-writing—the so-called well-made play—is not so rigid to-day as it was thirty years ago, when the drawing-room comedy or the thriller was almost the sole standard West End success. Eliot, Whiting, Fry, Bridie and Ustinov have broken the realistic barriers of the West End with plays which are not in the strict realistic convention and these plays have sometimes made money for their backers.

The insurance formula is also found in the architecture of the stage itself. This architecture to some extent conditions both play-writing, production and acting. The proscenium arch stage, resembling a picture frame, or a room from which the fourth wall has been removed, is only ideally suited to a particular kind of play-writing—those plays which might be called illusionist, being an imitation of life, or a mock reality. This peep-show architecture is not ideally suited to the epic plays of Greece, nor to Elizabethan plays, nor to any larger than life drama. If it be contended that such plays are not written to-day, we can only reply that parents consider it unwise to produce children until they can have a home to put them in.

In previous lectures in this University, Richard Southern expounded the doctrine of the open stage.* Most of us who have had opportunities of producing on such a stage, or have seen it in action, are reasonably convinced that development along the lines of the extended platform stage would give a fresh impetus to authorship, acting and design, and meet with more public approval than is generally supposed by the conservative critic.

We have only to see the way in which the audience have responded to the appeal of the show on ice, which, when presented in a skating rink, is a form of open-stage, or the popularity of the productions in the Assembly Hall at Edinburgh, or at Stratford, Ontario, or at the Maddermarket Theatre at Norwich, or the open-air productions of Avignon, York and Salzburg, to realise that the convention of Victorian theatrical architecture is by no means the only theatre that the ordinary citizen is prepared to accept.

The conservatism of the British theatre architecture is partly due to a mistaken belief that the public is more influenced by tradition than in fact it is. The public is prepared to accept any form of theatrical convention, providing that convention is capable of presenting plays in a manner which entertains. Clearly the open stage in many cases, though not all, is able to do so. But why should the London theatre abandon or alter its solidly built playhouses to indulge in an expensive, fanciful

* 'The Open Stage', by Richard Southern (Faber & Faber).

experiment, which is not required by the average type of play? I do not say it should, I only maintain it would be wise to experiment in new forms, and not rely exclusively on an artistic formula which is rapidly becoming sterile. The cinema and television have taken over from the theatre all the marvels of the illusionist technique. In the realm of realism and in the realm of fantasy, there is no trick or effect that is not better presented on the screen—be it wide angled or the miniature peepshow of the television cabinet. The Victorian theatre form was the pinnacle of stage realism, beyond which live drama cannot advance. An art form which has reached its zenith would be wise to find a new approach before it falls into a decline.

It is to be hoped that an enterprising manager will present an open-stage production as a commercial venture in the West End of London before too long; for there may be unsuspected prizes to be gained from the novelty thereby created, and the public interest engendered. For this purpose it might be necessary to commission a contemporary playwright, in much the same way as Eliot wrote *Murder in the Cathedral* for Canterbury. A successful commercial production of a play outside the conventional theatre buildings might do much to free the theatre of its realistic shackles and open up a new line of development for the stage architecture of the future.

British and American theatrical direction, in so far as they are represented by the theatre of the West End and of Broadway, tends to shut its eyes to the development that is going on around it. And from this point of view much good might be done by a more frequent interchange of directors between London and the Continent. Language difficulties are not a major stumbling block in all cases, as has been proved by excursions of British directors to direct plays in the native theatres of Helsinki, Stockholm, Holland and Tel-Aviv. Naturally, a British author would not be likely to agree to a foreign director for the first production of his new play, but revivals of Molière, Ibsen, Tchechov and Pirandello and new productions from Paris might gain much from the knowledge and new outlook of a native director. Both Kommisarjevsky and Michel St. Denis brought new life to the British stage, though neither was suitable for all types of British plays. The results of an interchange of directors with the Continent, as well as our present system of interchange with New York directors, would, I think, do much to vary the pattern of Anglo-American realism, and promote the same interest in theatrical art, as is promoted in the graphic arts by exhibitions of foreign painting and sculpture.

To sum up, we appear to have a chain of events controlling the London stage partly due to financial causes, and partly to an over-cautious estimate of public opinion, which latter cause is closely bound up with the former. The commercial manager who invests large sums of money in a production, either from his own funds or from his backer's, cannot risk experiments, nor does he feel encouraged to do so. He develops a cautious policy of playing for safety which is reflected in the type of theatre he builds and the type of play he encourages. The director, whose livelihood depends on the manager, reflects this mood in the type of scenery he commissions and the type of actors he engages. The author, though he may have broken away from the conventional subjects of the well-made play, cannot break away from the realistic treatment of his subject, unless encouraged to do so by the prospect of commercial production. And so the formula becomes almost inescapable. If the margin of profit between costs and receipts could be broadened, risks might be taken and theatrical direction liberated from its dangerously static condition. But this state of affairs can only come about by enlarging the theatre's audience, for no sane person believes that wages and prices will show an appreciable decline within foreseeable circumstances.

The problem, therefore, that confronts those of us who work in the theatre is not how to cut our costs, but how to increase our public. But before we consider how to tackle this problem, let us look outside London to see if we can find a less static condition in the provinces.

Behind the commercial theatre of London, and depending on it for existence, are the big touring theatres of the provinces, receiving their drama programme from the London companies who largely use this extension of their empire as try-out grounds for productions destined for the West End. Apart from dramatic try-outs, which are confined to a small number of cities, the rest of the provincial touring theatre trades in revues and revivals of musicals. The old touring drama of the actor-manager is almost entirely defunct, since the West End star can find more lucrative employment in films or radio work, which save him from the drudgery of travelling the country. Moreover, the secondary purpose of the old tours of a London success was to enhance the national prestige of the actor-manager and to provide him with a wider public. But this purpose, also, is better performed by the films and television. So to-day the provincial touring theatre is a shadow of its former self. No longer is a lively interest in the theatre built up by the tours of the great performances of the London theatre—an interest which did much to inspire many a young provincial to write or act for the stage. To-day the provincial public must be sufficiently well-off to travel to London to see first-class theatre, unless there is a major repertory in the town itself, or the town is lucky enough to draw the pre-London try-outs.

Outside the West End theatre and its provincial extension there is the repertory movement. But apart from the major repertory companies, which I will consider later, such as the Old Vic, Stratford, Birmingham, Glasgow, Liverpool and Bristol, the great majority of the reps. are even more precariously placed than the West End. By no stretch of imagination could they be regarded as flourishing concerns, either artistically or financially. In most cases they exist on a

6   81

shoe-string; and, having no reserves to meet the many setbacks which the theatre is bound to encounter, they live under constant threat of disaster. A run of failures, a prolonged spell of unpropitious weather, and the rep. is plunged in financial difficulties. To an even greater degree than the West End, the smaller repertory movement is forced to play for safety—choosing those plays which have already succeeded in London, and endeavouring, within limited means, to copy the formula of the London stage production. Can we look to these brave weekly and fortnightly repertories for the new blood we require? Alas, only to a limited extent. Their programme is too circumscribed, and their means too small, to encourage new writing or new staging. Only in so far as they give opportunities to young actors and technicians to develop experience and confidence can they claim to be advancing the cause of the theatre.

This is, however, a valuable contribution, although its value is limited. For young actors and actresses require a good deal of guidance in their early days; and this they are unlikely to obtain in the rushed conditions of rehearsal imposed by weekly and fortnightly changes of bill. Moreover, too often, experienced guidance is lacking; and the directors of these theatres are either too young themselves, or too hardened by the conditions of their work, to provide sympathetic and helpful training. Nevertheless, the experience of playing to a public, provided by our extensive repertory system, is one of the reasons why the general standard of supporting parts on the London stage is higher than that of New York, where the limited number of the summer stock theatres are almost the only opportunity for the younger American players to play large parts in front of a public. A national stage which depends exclusively on the metropolis for its existence, will tend to be starved of experienced performers in the all-important smaller roles.

There remains the amateur movement which in some cases

has adopted an adventurous production policy, though on the whole it is under the influence of the West End stage. But such experiments as the more adventurous amateurs are able to make are limited by their lack of training, which prevents their ideas from being shown off to the best advantage, and by their lack of good new plays; for the skilled author must earn his living by writing for the professionals.

To sum up, then, I suggest that the British theatre, in its endeavour to avoid taking risks, has clung too long to a safety-first policy. Unlike the other arts, it has not ventured into unexplored regions; it has remained in the rut of realism, from which it can develop no further. It is unfair to fix the blame for this too heavily on to any one side of the theatre complex. If the theatre was organised nationally, as it is in Eastern Europe, what was gained by the lowbrows, who profit on crooners, could be spent on experiment by the highbrows; but the theatre is not so organised in this country, and I don't advocate it ever should be. For although our British theatre is lacking in any comprehensive plan, it has within it the elements of a healthy existence. The West End theatre, whatever its drawbacks, is by virtue of its commercialism, providing a market for new plays. A competent playwright can derive a living from his royalties. As a result, we have in London and New York a reasonably large number of authors writing for the theatre, who might, under less commercial circumstances, have been drawn away into the cinema or journalism, or novel-writing. And we have, by virtue of the repertory system, a rudimentary training ground for actors and actresses. What we appear to lack is a more progressive spirit in the direction and scenic art of our theatre, and a more adventurous policy in encouraging a larger percentage of the public to visit it.

This survey is, however, incomplete without looking, first, at the club theatres of London, and second, at the major repertory theatres. In addition to the club theatres, such as the Arts Theatre and the New Lindsay, there are a number of try-out theatres, such as the Embassy, the Kew Theatre and the Lyric, Hammersmith. On the whole, these latter theatres are performing the function of the provincial try-out theatre, and although they do serve a local public, their principal task is to feed the West End stage. In consequence, we would not expect to find a highly original or individual style of production operating in them. The London club theatres—especially the Arts Theatre—are making a valuable contribution both to methods of staging and in the choice of repertoire, but their influence is bound to be limited by the size of their memberships and stages. It is in the major repertories that, I believe, the most significant and influential work is being done in the all-important task of maintaining public awareness of the theatre as a contemporary art. The two major repertories in the country are the Old Vic and the Shakespeare Memorial Theatre at Stratford. So far as we can generalise about a popular and a progressive style of direction, it could be said that, in the sphere of the classics, these two theatres are performing their function; though naturally they are bound to have their due measure of failure as well as success. On the whole it can be claimed that the directors in these theatres have, on the one hand, succeeded in breaking down the formula of realism which threatened to smother Shakespeare's stage-craft and, on the other, of avoiding the pitfalls of archaic reconstruction. But their choice of plays is now almost exclusively limited to Shakespeare, and the need for a theatre providing a more comprehensive classical repertoire is, I consider, pressing; though possibly it lies outside the scope of the Old Vic to embrace it. The work of Shakespeare strides, like a Colossus, across the path of our dramatic literature. Often his shadow seems a little oppressive, dwarfing other dramatists to such an extent that the public are unwilling to accept their plays when they are introduced into a repertoire side by side with Shakespeare. There is, I think, room for two National Theatre buildings in London; one for the production of Shakespeare, the other Elizabethan dramatists and Greek drama; and another for 18th-century drama and the more contemporary school of dramatic literature. It may well be that the Old Vic building can be incorporated into the National Theatre scheme in this way. The fact that the two theatres are not housed under one roof may prove a psychological advantage from the point of view of the smaller type of play—an advantage which would outweigh the administrative disadvantages of the separation of workshops and wardrobes. In much the same way, the Comédie Française have benefited from the separation of the Salle Richelieu, the home of Molière and the major classics, and the Salle Luxembourg which tends to favour a more contemporary repertoire.

In the other major repertory theatres we can see the development of a solid background to sustain and nourish the future of the Art of the Theatre. The remarkable record of Sir Barry Jackson's management of the Birmingham Repertory Theatre includes the first production of such plays as *Abraham Lincoln*, *The Barrets of Wimpole Street*, *The Farmer's Wife* and *Bird-in-Hand*, as well as several of Shaw's plays. No less remarkable is Birmingham's list of revivals of little known classics and translations of foreign plays. Liverpool, if it has not sponsored such an original list of plays as Birmingham, has trained some of the best talent amonst British actors and actresses. Glasgow is rightly making a corner in Scottish drama. Bristol, the youngest of the major repertories, has succeeded in establishing a name for itself, not only in the quality of its revivals, but also in bringing its wares to London.

Perhaps the major example of a native repertory theatre is the Abbey Theatre in Dublin, which has succeeded in developing an individual style of acting and production, as well as encouraging an outstanding dramatic literature of its own. The Abbey Theatre movement, however, is in no way linked to the British theatre, being a national theatre in its own right, but its influence on the Glasgow Citizen's Theatre, and on the growing importance of the Ulster Group Theatre, is discernible.

The importance of the major repertory companies is threefold; firstly, it is in these companies and in some of the smaller repertories as well, that new talent both in the form of players and technicians is being trained; secondly, their style of play-direction, particularly in the Old Vic, Stratford, Bristol and Birmingham, is often more progressive and less bound by the realistic formula than the West End; thirdly, by their very existence, they are increasing the public interest in, and knowledge of, the Art of the Theatre.

But we cannot afford to be complacent about the future of the theatre, as represented by the West End, on the one hand, and the major repertories, on the other. It is clear that, outside London on the one hand, and Stratford on the other, only a few provincial cities, with a population of a quarter of a million or over, can expect to see good theatre. It has been said that this is a not unreasonable state of affairs, and that in recent years the theatre has tried to spread its net too wide. Good theatre, like good music and good pictures, is an expensive commodity, and we cannot have an art gallery and a philharmonic orchestra in every village. But whilst a love for music and pictures can be inculcated, and to some extent satisfied, by the radio and the gramophone, for the one, and by comparatively inexpensive travelling exhibitions for the other; neither love for, nor understanding of, the peculiar qualities of live theatre can be satisfied by the television or the cinema which are entertainments in their own right, and cannot be regarded as substitutes for the living stage.

Now, although I believe the State and the local authorities should contribute to what we might call the higher branches of the live theatre, just as they do to the museums, art galleries, orchestras and swimming baths—and we must not forget that the cinema benefits through state loans and the radio through monopoly—yet, I do not believe the public authorities should be expected to support indefinitely a theatre which shows no intention of helping itself. The Arts Council has not the means to turn weekly repertories into three weekly repertories, or even fortnightly repertories. Nor do I believe that, even if such enormous funds were put at its disposal, it would be right to do so. There is no excuse for subsidising empty seats indefinitely.

We come back, therefore, to our remedy; it is not subsidies we want, nor higher prices, it is a larger audience. There seems to me little doubt that a potentially larger audience for the theatre exists; the extension of Secondary and University education is creating it, the B.B.C. and television are successfully exploiting it. The question of how the theatre is to reach it, is a question of tactics. What plan, then, can we make to convert the new potential audience outside the few major strongholds to the theatre?

The theatre must go out to meet the people, not sit back and wait for the people to come to it. Only a small fraction of the potential audience of to-day, which is spread throughout the length and breadth of the country, has ever seen good theatre. This potential public has seen touring revues, tired post-London musicals with second-class casts, and inadequate reps. on the one hand; and first-class performances on the cinema and television on the other. It is not surprising that the younger people choose the latter, and wonder why anyone should prefer the live theatre, which seems to be such poor entertainment.

During the war, when the Old Vic was damaged by enemy action, it sent out tours of plays, acted by competent and sometimes star casts, to the mining districts of Wales and the industrial towns of Northern England. These tours were not financially profitable, but the halls in which the plays were performed were packed, and an interest was engendered which unfortunately could not be developed. In France, where the theatre complex is similar to ours, the government have thought it worth while to sponsor, not only theatres in the large centres of population where a theatrical tradition exists, but touring theatres which go out to convert new audiences on their home ground. Such sponsored touring theatres must be prepared to do two things; firstly, to meet and explain themselves to this new audience in terms which that audience can understand; and secondly, to dispense with the conventional theatre buildings since these are not available to them. Firstly, then, these theatrical companies must be prepared to convert new audiences, and not merely rely on the old theatre habitués who are numerically insufficient to support it. The Théatre National Populaire of France does this by creating a general atmosphere of an event and of festival in the towns which it visits and by organising a wide-spread publicity campaign which does not rely solely on poster advertising. Secondly, the companies must stage their plays in new surroundings, making use of the techniques of the open or platform stage. Thirdly, they must select plays, or better still commission plays, which can be staged in non-realistic conditions in the guildhalls, in chapter houses of cathedrals, in roller-skating rinks, if necessary, and to stage them imaginatively, so that they are a fresh and vital entertainment to the public.

Is not this an opportunity for the research unit and the nation-wide publicity agency we are seeking? Is it not one opportunity to develop a new stage technique which would bring new blood to the tired formula of 19th-century convention? Is it not, also, an exciting stimulant to the actor and director, and above all, to the author? Let me say briefly how I see such a touring theatre operating.

Firstly, I must point out that I am not considering a poverty-stricken, fit-up theatre playing in some draughty hall in the outer suburbs. I am considering a high-standard company, complete with its own mobile platform stage, playing in the centre of a town's normal activity. The visit of such a company must be made an event in the life of the town, much the same sort of event as must have been created by the strolling players of the 16th century, who were not afraid of beating the drum round the town, or as was created by the touring theatre of Henry Irving and of the other actor-managers, who understood the value of a hard-working and efficient advance-publicity manager.

Secondly, I do not advocate that such a theatre should operate in towns which already possess a good repertory or a first-class touring theatre, for its purpose would not be to compete with what exists, but to convert those who have no opportunity of seeing good theatre.

Thirdly, I do not consider that a high standard can be maintained if such a theatre plays for less than a week in each centre, for the players must rehearse their production, and they cannot do that if they spend all their time in railway carriages or buses.

Fourthly, I do not suggest that this theatre should play in towns where there is an insufficiently large population to fill the seats for one week. As I see it, each of these touring companies should operate in four centres with populations ranging between 70,000 and 200,000 so that each centre receives a visit from its company on a regular basis of one week in each month. It would probably be wise to cease activity during the summer and to attempt no more than an eight months' season. Each company would, therefore, present no more than eight plays a year, which is about as much as a company can be expected to do, if a high standard is to be maintained. This restricted season is in itself a spur to the public's interest, and eight plays a year is not too much to inculcate that sense of an event that we are seeking. The theatre must not be regarded as a commonplace, if it is to be stimulating.

It may be argued that actors are too smug to undertake such pilgrimages. It is true that star actors would be unlikely to make such a sacrifice, but it is also true that unemployment in the theatre is at present about 40 per cent. of the membership of Equity (3,000 actors and actresses per week). The young actor

89

*on this leader
The Director*

to-day demands neither great rewards nor luxurious conditions; he is ready to pioneer for his experience, but he does
demand inspiring leadership; that is where the director comes
in.

It may be argued that such tours are too costly. Experiments
in touring repertory have been tried before and have generally
proved to be so. The Young Vic and the Salisbury Arts Theatre
had to be withdrawn for financial reasons. But the Salisbury
experiment was based on small centres of population (Salisbury
itself has a population of 30,000), and the Young Vic, which
had a tremendously stimulating influence, covered too wide
an area for continuity of interest to be built up. But there are
other touring repertories still in existence, and even if these
have not reached the high standard of performance we are
seeking—for the standards must not be lower than the best
major repertories—they have proved that there is a demand for
theatre, even if the smaller centres they visit are not sufficiently
large to make such visits profitable.

But the scheme I am advocating envisages a wider purpose
than the conventional touring repertory based on theatre
buildings. It envisages the development of new roads along
which the future theatre can travel, better able to meet the
competition of other entertainment; it envisages converting
new audiences to the theatre by restoring to it that sense of an
event which the small repertories are unable to provide. It is
true that such theatres would be unlikely to cover their costs—
at least for some years—but it depends on how we look at this
question of finance. If, in fact, such theatres can be the real
experimental department we are seeking; an experimental department which stages its plays in a new way because it has to,
instead of staging them in a new way in order to be highbrow;
if, in fact, such theatres are increasing the potential audience
for the future, introducing new talent to the theatre, and encouraging new ways of writing, is it after all more costly than
bolstering up theatres which are imitating the old formula

of success? I am not suggesting that the smaller reps. be abandoned by the public authority or by any other patron who is generous enough to support them. But I believe that the Arts Council, together with the civic and municipal authorities, should examine the possibilities of an adventurous touring scheme which would foster good theatre in the theatreless towns, instead of relying on the spasmodic and unco-ordinated efforts of companies that are insufficiently financed and lacking in experienced direction. Such a scheme for touring theatres, covering the larger cities which are unable to support a three-weekly repertory, would be complementary to the project for strengthening the position of the major repertories outlined by the Secretary General of the Arts Council in the two Shute lectures he delivered at Liverpool in 1953. If we could have a network of good theatres outside London, covering the major cities by means of the static repertory system, and the lesser cities by means of the touring repertory, we would, I believe, establish a sound foundation for the theatre of the future, and provide the public with that sense of values in theatrical art which are at present so seriously lacking.

I suggest it is a sensible policy for the theatre to foster a progressive movement for its future welfare, and to advertise its best wares throughout the country. It is not in London, where there are over forty theatres, that money should be spent on experiment and research, but in the provinces, which in the main have no adequate theatrical life of their own, and where improvisation and experiment are necessary.

A greater contribution to the theatre is probably being made by the productions at Stratford, Ontario, than in any London or provincial repertory theatre since William Poel, Granville Barker and Gordon Craig revolutionised the theatre of the actor-managers. The director of to-day might do well to consider whether the greatest service he can render to the theatre and to the public does not lie in such fields of discovery. We might wonder how it is that a little town like Stratford in

Canada, with a population of 19,000, should consider it worth its while to sponsor an experiment of this nature. Perhaps the answer is that the public in the smaller cities has more faith in, and love for, good theatre than our public authorities believe. Perhaps the convention of 19th-century theatre—a convention which was good for its own age, but no longer corresponds to the new and exciting era into which we are entering—could be discarded more safely than we imagine. I call upon the director to meet with imagination and initiative, the exciting possibilities of the new and vital audience of the future.

Contemporary Shakespeare Production

*A Lecture for the Bergen Foundation, delivered at
Yale University on May 6th, 1954*

I PROPOSE to discuss the problem of contemporary
Shakespeare production by endeavouring to answer three
questions; firstly, how does the production of Shakespeare's
plays differ from that of a modern play? Secondly, what are the
main principles which should govern the director's approach?
Thirdly, what is the ideal way of staging these plays to-day?

It may seem to you that I have framed the first question
arbitrarily. Are the problems of directing a Shakespeare play
in fact any more severe than those of directing any play written
in a past age? Taste in theatrical fare changes almost as frequently as Paris fashions. To-day we prefer plays of psychology, more especially if they satisfy our obsession with our
guilt complex and are written in what passes for poetry.
Twenty years ago it was plays of high society and detective
fiction. To bridge the gap of time and make the theatrical
taste of an earlier age acceptable to a contemporary public is
always a problem for the director, but, although changes of
taste are sometimes a problem in presenting Shakespeare's
plays to a contemporary public, time has played an even
stranger trick with the major plays of Shakespeare, which

have become, by the very fact of their familiarity, a sort of sacrosanct ritual. It is the very fact that the taste of the contemporary public has been so strongly formed for Shakespeare's plays that creates its particular problem.

Every school child—not only those who share our own commonwealth of language, but in almost every country of the world—has been saturated in Shakespeare; and although many dislike him intensely as a result, not a few retain or develop a taste for his plays in adult life. These it is who form a critical section of the audience. Each of these brain-washed admirers has developed a certain prejudice about how Shakespeare's plays should be performed. Each has his own idea of *Macbeth* and *Hamlet*, of *Twelfth Night* and *As You Like It*. This idea may have been formed by the illustrations in some picture-book, or by the opinion of one of the legion of literary scholars who delve and prod around his plays, or by the influence of some particularly powerful performance he has seen on the stage, the films or television. The variety of means of propagating a taste for Shakespeare has resulted in a variety of opinions about how his plays should be performed, and no director can hope to satisfy such diversity of prejudice. In fact, he must not attempt to do so, for his work must be an expression of his own prejudice, not that of others.

Now, in dealing with a new play or a little-known revival, such prejudices do not exist, and, in consequence, the audience accepts without a struggle the director's interpretation of the script. Moreover, this intense indoctrination of Shakespeare has robbed the director and the actors of all power to surprise the audience with the development of the action and of any curiosity or suspense in the outcome of events. We all know Macbeth will murder Duncan and, though we may be interested in the actor's treatment of the hesitancy in performing this act, we are not—as was Shakespeare's audience—placed in a state of suspense to know the outcome of this struggle between Macbeth and his conscience. We not only know that

Othello will stab himself, but most of us know at what precise moment in his speech he will do so; and as for Hamlet, we can complete most of his lines before the actor has got half-way through them.

Familiarity with the text and the action not only robs the play of any possibility of surprising a large section of its audience, but it can produce restlessness amongst a sophisticated public if the situation is not treated with some measure of originality by the director, or if the performances given by the actors are not of a very high standard indeed. In fact the director of Shakespeare is faced with a far more critical public than is the director of a modern play or of almost any other play of the past. To overcome this familiarity with the text, the director is severely tempted to search for too great a novelty in his approach, and this is in itself a considerable danger—responsible for much of the monstrous perversion which goes under the name of Shakespearean direction.

Now although I would agree that every performance of Shakespeare should be treated creatively, and directed in such a way that it is in tune with the fashion and taste of its age, yet we must bear in mind that the ritualistic quality with which the great masterpieces of the theatre have become endowed provides its own power to move and excite the traditionalist section of the audience, and this section will be disturbed by any novelties introduced by the director. Even the fact that Alec Guinness wore a beard as Hamlet provoked a storm of criticism. In fact the Shakespeare 'fans' do not go to see *Hamlet* or *King Lear*, *Twelfth Night* or *Macbeth* to be entertained by the dramatic story alone, they go because from the unfolding of the familiar ritual they derive a spiritual satisfaction. How often when we hear a Shakespeare play performed do we suddenly experience a thrill of pleasure as we hear some familiar passage; how lovable are our favourite characters; what a special hush falls over the audience as we see Juliet come out upon the balcony and lean her cheek upon her hand. All this is part of the ritual, arising directly from familiarity with the plays. So that the director is faced with the delicate problem of balancing his conception of the play in such a way that, whilst it is in tune with the fashion and taste of its age, it loses nothing of its ritualistic power to move and excite the traditionalists.

But despite this ritualistic power and despite the considerable idolisation of this playwright, there are certain situations in his plays and certain facets of his stage-craft which are not easily acceptable to-day unless they are skilfully handled by the director. We have been brought up to believe that Shakespeare wrote for all ages and for all men, but this is one of those grandiloquent statements that sound very impressive, but require a little qualification. Shakespeare wrote for the taste of his own times and for the conditions of his own theatre, and these times and that theatre are very different from our own. An audience, part of whom stood in an open yard, often drenched by rain or stamping its feet against the cold, demanded a far more violent form of drama than does an audience comfortably seated in a centrally heated and air-conditioned theatre. It is significant that many of us find it preferable to read his plays than to see them on the stage. Is this not because many of his situations and effects are less crude when treated as literature than when performed as action?

The bloody head of Macbeth spiked on a pole, the piled up corpses at the end of *Hamlet*, the ghosts who constantly arrive at the most inconvenient moments, those tiresome witches and their apparitions, the unspeakable barbarities of *Titus Andronicus*, the callous behaviour of Claudio to Hero—all these and many more examples could be quoted of the change in theatrical taste between Shakespeare's audience and the audience of to-day.

Whilst indulging in our sentimental memories of the exquis-ite beauty of Shakespeare's poetry, we sometimes forget the fact that he was, by our standards, a crude and often coarse writer. If any argument is needed to support the fact that these plays were written by an untutored genius, a self-educated country man, and not by the scholarly and aristocratic pretenders who have been advanced by the literary detectives, surely the coarseness of the jests, the naivety of historical knowledge, the errors in taste, the anachronisms, the superstitious credulity in ghosts and magic are proof in themselves that the author of these plays was no fine gentleman nor well-read University wit. Would Bacon or Oxford or Derby have descended to such blood-curdling melodrama as the banquet in *Titus Andronicus*, in which a mother eats her two sons baked in a pie, or such coarse jests as those indulged in by Lavache in *All's Well That Ends Well*? Such rough magic, which charmed the prentice boys of the pit and incurred the strong displeasure of the magistrates and the preachers during Shakespeare's lifetime, can, unless skilfully handled, appear distasteful, or ludicrous to our taste to-day. And, whilst it is not my intention to magnify the contribution the director makes to the appreciation of Shakespeare in the theatre, nor to minimise his greatness as a playwright, I would suggest that there are more problems involved in mounting Shakespeare's plays, than are likely to come the way of a director of a modern play. I would add that there are also deeper satisfactions.

But the principal difference between Shakespeare's theatre and our own is the difference between the theatre building for which he wrote and that in which we most commonly perform. This difference extends not only to the question of scenery, costumes, lighting, but to the form in which the plays were constructed.

We are all sufficiently aware of the architectural difference between Shakespeare's Globe and our contemporary pictorial stage. The principle of our pictorial stage, which we have inherited from a tradition foreign to Shakespeare, is that it seeks to satisfy our increased taste for visual effects. It is a sort of magician's cabinet, whose displays are revealed to the audience by the opening of the curtain. The technique of opening and closing the cabinet cuts the play up into a series of tableaux or scenes, each representing realistically or by strong visual indication a definite locality. The writers who cater for it have, therefore, constructed their plays with an eye to its peculiarities, and have so arranged their action that their plays do not suffer from being treated as a series of chapters. As a result of the gain in pictorial effect has come a corresponding loss in the use of the spoken word. No longer is it necessary to create mood and location by descriptive language, since these can be more easily suggested by scenic illusion and lighting.

Look for instance at the difference between Shakespeare's method of treating a dramatic sequence and that of a later age. This is how the Chorus of *Henry V* describes the passage of the English fleet across the Channel to Harfleur:

> O, do but think
> You stand upon the rivage and behold
> A city on the inconstant billows dancing;
> For so appears this fleet majestical,
> Holding due course to Harfleur. Follow, follow:

And contrast this passage with the following description taken from the London *Times* of 1839, showing how Macready treated this sequence:

'This third act was ushered in by a moving diorama, by far the most splendid piece of scenery presented on this occasion. The English Fleet is seen leaving Southampton, its course is traced across the sea, and the audience are gradually brought to the siege of Harfleur.'

Recently we have seen how this same situation was treated even more pictorially in Laurence Olivier's film of the play.

Now since to receive an impression through the eye requires less effort and is, on the whole, more immediately effective than to receive it through the ear, an audience that has witnessed a fully pictorialised performance of Shakespeare will not readily accept, as a popular form of entertainment, the bare stage and crude machinery of the Elizabethan playhouse. The magic of the spoken word, though it is still potent, is not by itself enough to qualify as theatrical entertainment to-day.

This emphasis on visual effect is seen in nearly all means of contemporary communication; it is a taste which cannot readily be ignored. Sound radio is rapidly disappearing before television; the black and white talkie to the greater visual effect of the coloured cinemascope; the film is encroaching on the school-teacher; the strip-cartoon on the story-writer. So that, although the permanent features of the Elizabethan stage may have been a sufficient background for Shakespeare's audience, to-day we require a greater degree of decorative effect and at least some indication of a change of scene.

Now although it is true that Shakespeare's plays appear in most of the earliest versions to have been divided up into some kind of rudimentary scene and act divisions, many of these have been inaccurately imposed by the printer. This very inaccuracy indicates the unimportance of these divisions. A modern printer even if he was pirating a play by Shaw would have no doubt where the scenes ended. Shakespeare's scene divisions had clearly nothing like the finality of those of a contemporary play; in any case the multiplicity of the scenes—in *Antony and Cleopatra* there are twenty-two—prevents the director from treating each as a complete chapter. Yet, since he is forced by the taste of his age and the architectural nature of his theatre to give to each scene some kind of pictorial distinction, we can see how his difficulties begin to mount,

So we can say that, apart from the handicap of familiarity with the plays and the need to treat them as ritual, there are additional problems of taste and pictorial representation which constitute the gap between the Shakespeare play and the modern stage. It is this gap which the director must bridge. On the one hand he will find no honest solution if he attempts to modernise the plays—if he alters the text or substitutes revolvers for rapiers; on the other, he will achieve no more than academic interest or temporary curiosity if he tries to imitate the past—if he rebuilds the Globe, surrounds it with olde worlde ale-houses—no, not even if he forces his audience to wear trunks and farthingales.

We cannot relive the past and Shakespeare's theatre is buried deep beneath the turmoil of a new and different age. How strangely prophetic are Prospero's words:

> ' . . . These our actors
> As I foretold you, were all spirits, and
> Are melted into air, into thin air:
> And like the baseless fabric of this vision,
> The cloud-capp'd towers, the gorgeous palaces,
> The solemn temples, the great globe itself,
> Yes, all which it inherit, shall dissolve,
> And like this insubstantial pageant faded,
> Leave not a rack behind.'

Shakespeare's Globe has dissolved, and to try to reproduce what happened there is now but the baseless fabric of a vision. The problem we face is how to build a bridge which can span the river of time between him and us.

What, then, are the main principles of Shakespearean direction to which we must at all costs hold fast?

First amongst these is the question of continuity of action which arises from the question I have already indicated: namely, what value we should place on Shakespeare's scenic division?

Since the 18th century until comparatively recently, it was the custom to divide Shakespeare's plays up into a number of tableaux presenting visual pictures of battlements, throne rooms, prisons, forests, graveyards, streets and battlefields, all more or less realistically represented. By this division into scenes, the craftsmen of the pictorial theatre attempted to squeeze the Elizabethan Leviathan into the conventions of their own stage. Superb scenic effects were created: real waterfalls splashed and tame rabbits flopped amongst the scenery of Tree's production of *A Midsummer Night's Dream*: a herd of deer grazed in the Forest of Arden, whilst Cleopatra appeared in a barge, surrounded by virgins and eunuchs, the very magnificence of which completely negatived Enobarbus' description. But these spectacular orgies often entailed long waits between scenes whilst the next tableau was set, and resulted in disjointed, cumbersome entertainment which, though it might satisfy the craving for visual spectacle, destroyed the flow of the play.

Now this flow, I maintain, is of the utmost importance and to destroy it is to destroy one of the major effects of his plays upon an audience. If spectacular or realistic production is aimed at—even when aided by revolving stages, by lifts or projected backgrounds—the flow of the play is bound to suffer: the action becomes disjointed and the audience's judgement is influenced, not so much by the content of the scene, as by its pictorial presentation. The mighty impulse of event flowing on to event is lost, and it is this impulse which creates the unity of the play, and which holds the rapt attention of the spectator riveted upon the stage. Once concentrated attention—that magic link between stage and auditorium—is broken by the dropping of a curtain and the twittering of an orchestra, the audience loses touch with the play; and, however small the break of concentration may be, it is sufficient to destroy the cumulative effect.

The director's problem is how to achieve pictorial effects without disturbing the cumulative flow. I can offer no general solution to this problem, which must depend on the arrangement of each play's action. In some plays the problem is not so difficult—the greater part of *A Midsummer Night's Dream* takes place in the forest and only very little scenery need be added to suggest the Palace of Theseus. *Love's Labour's Lost* can be played satisfactorily in three locations with two convenient intervals to effect the change of scene. The Roman plays can often be effectively staged with a permanent arrangement of pillars and rostra with removable pieces to mark different locations.

In other plays the problem is more difficult—*The Merry Wives of Windsor* for instance seems to me to need a fairly solid construction with doors and windows to serve for its interior and exterior sequences—a construction that might be best supplied by using an adaptation of the Elizabethan tiring-house, with its balcony and understage; but then comes the problem of the last scene in Windsor Forest for which this construction is hopelessly inadequate. Nearly every play has similar problems. *Hamlet* would be simple enough to stage were it not for the graveyard; *Antony and Cleopatra* has the problem of the monument which can be a thorough nuisance if it is on the stage all the time; *Romeo and Juliet* its tomb interior and its balcony; *The Tempest* its sinking ship; *Lear* and *Macbeth* their blasted heaths.

The second major principle is that of the style of acting and speaking the lines. In considering this question we are dealing as much with the actors as with the director, but it is the director's responsibility to choose actors who are sufficiently experienced and sufficiently sensitive to speak the prose with style and the verse with poetic appreciation.

But good verse speaking is not enough; to it must be added the qualities of what is currently regarded as good acting. In the 18th and early 19th centuries, good acting was considered to consist primarily of a magnetic presence, an ability to display emotion through gesture and grimace, and a powerful and well-modulated voice. In such conditions the task of acting Shakespeare was perhaps easier than it is to-day, when the emphasis of acting is much more on the naturalistic approach to a part than on the histrionic approach of the classical and romantic actors. I doubt very much if our modern critics would

praise the acting of Kean and Sarah Siddons; they would consider them as outsize personalities who disregarded all attempts
at naturalistic behaviour. This emphasis on the realistic in acting is a comparatively new fashion, which the director can no
more afford to ignore than he can the public preference that
female parts in Shakespeare should be played by actresses instead of boys. He must then, ally the audience's taste for this
contemporary fashion for naturalistic acting with fine verse
speaking—a delicate adjustment, because the two approaches
are often, though not always, at war with each other.

Rhetorical passages such as Antony's speech to the Roman
citizens over Caesar's body, or Henry V's speech at Agincourt
can be integrated into a realistic performance, since they are
intended as oratory, but difficulties arise when the modern
actor tries to adjust his realistic approach to the reflective soliloquies of Hamlet, Timon and Macbeth. The modern actor will
argue that a man beset by thoughts of suicide does not deliver
the soliloquy of 'To be or not to be' with special emphasis on
its poetic quality, but speaks it in disjointed sentences and treats
it rather as subconscious muttering than as blank verse. This
gap between our current taste for psychological realism and
our undeveloped technique for poetic speech is one of the difficult problems that the modern director has to bridge. But
whatever the demand may be for naturalistic acting, the director must hold fast to the poetic style, for without it the play
loses all magic.

The director must realise that a great part of Shakespeare's
speech, whether it be poetry or prose is verbal music. It requires
much the same orchestration from the actors as does a sym-
phony by Beethoven or an opera by Mozart. Much of *Love's
Labour's Lost* is unintelligible to us to-day, and if we treat the
speech realistically the audience will speedily abandon any
attempt to listen to such apparent gibberish. But the magic of
this play is not its intellectual content, which is in any case
small, but its musical content. Once we treat it as verbal music,

once we give value to its cadenzas and scherzos, its andantes and largos, we create aural entertainment of a very high order.

Consider this verbal aria from *Love's Labour's Lost*, where Biron persuades the King of Navarre and his fellow bachelors to abandon their scholarly monastic existence and become lovers:

'O, we have made a vow to study, lords,
And in that vow we have forsworn our books.
For when would you, my liege, or you, or you,
In leaden contemplation have found out
Such fiery numbers as the prompting eyes
Of beauty's tutors have enrich'd you with?
Other slow arts entirely keep the brain;
And therefore, finding barren practisers,
Scarce show a harvest of their heavy toil:
But love, first learned in a lady's eyes,
Lives not alone immured in the brain;
But, with the motion of all elements,
Courses as swift as thought in every power,
And gives to every power a double power,
Above their functions and their offices.
It adds a precious seeing to the eye;
A lover's eyes will gaze an eagle blind;
A lover's ear will hear the lowest sound,
When the suspicious head of theft is stopp'd:
Love's feeling is more soft and sensible
Than are the tender horns of cockled snails;
Love's tongue proves dainty Bacchus gross in taste;
For valour is not Love a Hercules,
Still climbing trees in the Hesperides?
Subtle as Sphinx; as sweet and musical
As bright Apollo's lute, strung with his hair;
And when Love speaks, the voice of all the gods
Makes heaven drowsy with the harmony. . . .'

Or consider this passage from *As You Like It* beween Silvius,

Phebe, Orlando and Rosalind. Did ever words approach so closely to a part-song?

PHE.	Good shepherd, tell this youth what 'tis to love.
SIL.	It is to be all made of sighs and tears;
	And so am I for Phebe.
PHE.	And I for Ganymede.
ORL.	And I for Rosalind.
ROS.	And I for no woman.
SIL.	It is to be all made of faith and service;
	And so am I for Phebe.
PHE.	And I for Ganymede.
ORL.	And I for Rosalind.
ROS.	And I for no woman.
SIL.	It is to be all made of fantasy,
	All made of passion, and all made of wishes;
	All adoration, duty, and observance,
	All humbleness, all patience, and impatience,
	All purity, all trial, all observance;
	And so am I for Phebe.
PHE.	And so am I for Ganymede.
ORL.	And so am I for Rosalind.
ROS.	And so am I for no woman.
PHE.	If this be so, why blame you me to love you?
SIL.	If this be so, why blame you me to love you?
ORL.	If this be so, why blame you me to love you?
ROS.	Who do you speak to, 'Why blame you me to love you?'
ORL.	To her that is not here, nor doth not hear.

Like the problem of continuity of action, Shakespeare relies upon verbal music as an integral part of his stage-craft.

The third principle to which the director of Shakespeare must hold fast is the balance of characterisation. Shakespeare's plays have for too long been considered as vehicles for the apotheosis of star actors, rather than as closely integrated company plays which they were meant to be. This danger is less acute to-day than it was in the days of the actor-managers who cut and rearranged the texts in order to emphasise the importance of their own performance; perhaps because our star performers are more intellectually minded than their ancestors, and have a greater appreciation of the value of the so-called minor parts. But there is much still to be found in the minor roles that can contribute to the value of the plays' themes. Rosencrantz and Guildernstern, Salanio and Salerino, Gloucester and Edmund, Nym and Bardolph, the servants and messengers, the country folk and the clowns, repay better casting than they sometimes get. A production of *Love's Labour's Lost*, for which I was responsible, won some praise from the critics owing to the unsuspected values revealed in the parts of Holofernes and Sir Nathaniel as played by two of our most accomplished actors. I remember with gratitude the wonderful lift given to *Henry IV Part II* at the Old Vic by Laurence Olivier in the small part of Justice Shallow, and by Paul Scofield as the Young Clown in the Stratford production of *A Winter's Tale*. But the question of giving due value to the minor parts is also bound up with the question of tempo. The modern audience is so anxious to remain no more than two and three-quarter hours in the theatre that there is often little time left to develop such characters.

In considering the question of tempo and pace, which I might call the fourth principle of Shakespearean production, we are amazed to hear from the Chorus of *Romeo and Juliet* that the playing time is meant to take no more than two hours. Even allowing for poetic licence in this statement, an uncut performance of the play to-day would take three and a quarter hours with two ten-minute intervals and no unreasonable pauses for scene changes. Are we then to suppose that the speed of modern performances is much slower than Shakespeare intended? I think so. 'Speak the speech I pray you, as I pronounced it to you, trippingly on the tongue.' I believe that in our desire to achieve realistic acting we have largely lost the trick of speaking the speech trippingly. The only example I can quote of an actor who is capable of so doing is John Gielgud, who alone among his contemporaries, seems able to combine poetry, psychology and pace—the three p's that should be the motto of every contemporary Shakespearean player. To put it bluntly, if the leading actors can be encouraged to get a move on with their death scenes and cut out their psychological pauses, more time could be found to give effective emphasis to the minor characters.

I have now dealt with what I consider to be the main principles of Shakespearean production—continuity of action, poetic style, the balance of the performances and pace; it is now time for us to turn to the last of the questions which I posed at the beginning of this lecture, namely, what are the ideal conditions for staging a Shakespeare play?

Bearing in mind the principles that I have already outlined, we need firstly, a permanent or semi-permanent setting, sufficiently decorative to satisfy contemporary visual requirements and sufficiently flexible to allow changes of location to be indicated without breaking the flow of the action. I have said that there can be no hard and fast rules of how to achieve these changes, for the arrangement of the staging must depend on the play itself; but I would suggest that it is better to achieve them simply than to use elaborate mechanical devices. Shakespeare's stage-craft is a mixture of realism and imagination. His characters are real men and women, but they often speak in poetry, whilst his action fluctuates between actuality and phantasy—between the homespun reality of Bottom, the Weaver, and the cobweb world of Oberon and Titania. Too great an emphasis on the machine can destroy the imaginative response of the audience, for the audience must be encouraged to use its imagination, must be conditioned to react and respond to the magic of words, and not lulled into a mood of receiving entertainment without working for it.

In a production of *The Merchant of Venice* for which I was responsible at the Old Vic, I managed the alternation of Venice and Belmont by raising a white-columned pavilion on a lift, which rose out of the ground to represent Belmont. Although this device was decorative and did not interrupt the flow of scene into scene, since the actors were able to enter and start the next scene whilst the pavilion was rising or sinking; yet it had an element of contrivance about it—the audience were more interested in the machine than they were in the opening and closing lines of the scene.

On the whole the simplest means of changing the aspect of the scene are the best. It is more acceptable for the actors to bring on the necessary furniture or make slight scenic alterations themselves, and it is more in keeping with Shakespeare's stage-craft than elaborate mechanism.

The second ideal condition for the production of Shakespeare is to have some form of apron stage or projecting platform. The most satisfactory stage for Shakespeare, and, indeed, for all pre-Restoration drama, is the open platform stage, surrounded on three sides by the audience, devoid of a proscenium arch and of its traditional curtain. Once Shakespeare's plays are released from the restrictions of the baroque Italian tradition, with its illusionary and realistic associations, they assume a mobility and a three-dimension quality, which are lacking in the peep-show architecture of our conventional theatre buildings. Moreover, the audience will approach the production in a mood more receptive to the spoken word, and less demanding of scenic illusion. Examples of Shakespeare performances on such a stage can be seen at the annual Edinburgh Festival, where the Old Vic have staged *Romeo and Juliet*, *Hamlet* and *Macbeth* in the Assembly Hall, and at the tent theatre at Stratford, Ontario. This latter theatre is, I believe, the most satisfying experiment in contemporary Shakespeare theatre architecture that has yet been evolved. The auditorium is based on the semi-circular Greek tradition with its stepped seating, surrounding a projecting stage on three sides. The stage is built on varying levels, incorporating a balcony and side entrances. It possesses advantages over the Elizabethan stages, as far as our knowledge of these edifices extends, in that the balcony and under-balcony are in reasonable relationship to the audience, and can be used for intimate scenes without a vast area of unoccupied stage intervening between the players and the public. It has always been a mystery to me to know how Burbage and Shakespeare performed the tomb scene in *Romeo and Juliet* in the area under the balcony—which is generally held to be the acting area for all set interior scenes—if the proportions of the Elizabethan platform stage and the general shape of the auditorium were those that modern scholars have deduced. If Juliet's tomb was, in fact, discovered under the balcony on such a stage, then it was not only out of sight to quite a large number of spectators in the side balconies, but was too far removed, by the large area of unoccupied platform, to permit of the necessary actor-audience relationship which any experienced director knows to be essential.

The stage at Stratford, Ontario, has successfully overcome this problem; and possibly overcome it in a way which Burbage and his fellows would envy. But the adoption of the open stage should not, in my opinion, rule out some degree of scenic representation. Although no major difficulties occur with a simplified representation of courts, streets and private apartments—and the open stage easily lends itself to a feast of spectacle and movement in processions and battles—difficulties are bound to occur in the magic scenes of forest and glade, in such plays as *A Midsummer Night's Dream*, *As You Like It*, *Love's Labour's Lost*, and the final scene of *The Merry Wives of Windsor*. Lighting can do much to overcome the difficulty; so, too, can the use of imaginative simplicity by a few well chosen, and easily removable, properties. In a production of *A Midsummer Night's Dream* at the Darmstadt Staat's Theater, directed by Gustav Sellner, the fairies instantly transformed a bare stage into a leafy glade, by each bringing on enormous plastic leaves mounted on wire stands with them. The effect was not realistic, but completely satisfying in its atmospheric effect. This is the sort of magic which the contemporary director of Shake-speare must aim at. The trick can, perhaps, only be performed once; but the challenge to find a new and exciting way to overcome the difficulty of satisfying the audience without detracting from the flow of the play, or gilding the lily of the spoken description of the scene, is a challenge which the direc-tor must be prepared to meet.

The third condition, perhaps the most important, is to have a company of actors trained, or capable of being trained, to manage the words; to speak them intelligently, quickly, and with poetic rhythm. It only remains to add the obvious—namely that the best results will come from a team of actors who are used to playing Shakespeare together, such as the Old Vic or Stratford-on-Avon, than from selected performers, however talented, who have been brought together for a special production.

Lastly, there is the director himself, who, so far as Shake-spearean production is concerned, seems almost invariably to be regarded as a major criminal by dramatic critics. He is responsible for all these things: for stage and actors, for scenery, poetry and pace. He must be capable of appreciating the inten-tion of the playwright and, whilst presenting intact all that is characteristic and basic in his stage-craft ,he must solve the prob-lem of how to translate it into the contemporary theatre. On the intellectual side, he must so adjust his production that the difference of outlook between one age and the other does not mar or weaken the enjoyment of the play, and at the same time he must give due emphasis to the ritualistic qualities which the plays have come to assume in the minds of the audience. Lastly, if his production is to capture popular favour, it must be suffi-ciently original to overcome our familiarity with the text and yet not so original as to shock our preconceived idea of how the play should be performed.

Quite a formidable task, quite a considerable need for experi-ence and ability, for patience and courage. Perhaps that is why we rarely see a performance of Shakespeare in a modern theatre that wholly satisfies us. If we are to accept the fact that Shakespeare wrote for all ages and for all men, I submit that, although the universality of his genius is unquestionable, those three hundred and fifty years that separate us from him require a mighty well-made bridge and a deal of skilful manipulation to allow the vehicle of his genius to cross over the river of time and arrive undamaged on our contemporary shore.

I am conscious of the fact that I have only touched on the fringe of the problems raised by Shakespeare's stage-craft. I do not believe that we shall ever know enough about its mysteries to solve all our problems. I believe that Shakespeare, as a man of the theatre, would not have us waste too much time in probing the past, but rather that we should try to make his plays relive in terms of the present. When the great Globe itself dissolved in fire, his prompt books curled up and their grey ash rose upwards with its smoke.

> . . . . I have bedimm'd
> The noontide sun, call'd forth the mutinous winds,
> And 'twixt the green sea and the azured vault
> Set roaring war: to the dread rattling thunder
> Have I given fire, and rifted Jove's stout oak
> With his own bolt; the strong-based promontory
> Have I made shake, and by the spurs pluck'd up
> The pine and cedar: graves at my command
> Have waked their sleepers, oped, and let 'em forth
> By my so potent art. But this rough magic
> I here abjure. . . . I'll break my staff,
> Bury it certain fathoms in the earth,
> And deeper than did ever plummet sound
> I'll drown my book.